PRAISE FOR *UNLIKE JESUS*

As followers of Christ, we might know the message of God's love and forgiveness, but we have no one to tell because we are so unlike Jesus. Dr. Larry Dixon has clearly (and humorously) highlighted one of the greatest weaknesses in the Western Church today — we fail to develop friendships with outsiders. If David and Wayne had avoided me during our college days, I wonder how long it would have taken me to learn how to have a personal relationship with our Father God. I have known Dr. Dixon for decades and have watched him put the lessons of his book into practice. Read along and learn how to be much more like Jesus when it comes to sharing the greatest message on earth.

Dr. Bill Jones
Past President and Current Chancellor
Columbia International University

If anyone can speak to a creative and practical approach to connecting and relating to people, especially those who have no faith or church orientation, it's Larry Dixon. *Unlike Jesus...* will mess with your heart and mind. And that's why every Christ-follower should read this book.

Dr. David Olshine
Professor of Youth ministry, Family and Culture
Columbia International University
Founder of Youth Ministry Coaches
Speaker and Author

Like his other books, Dr. Dixon's newest book, *Unlike Jesus: Let's Stop Unfriending the World*, is Biblical, profound and, at the same time, refreshing and fun. And like his other books, this one is an "attack of sanity" for believers. Before you pray for the lost, witness to unbelievers or evangelize sinners, read this book. It will be the difference between wasting your time and seeing more "fruit" than you would believe. This book is a gift to Christians and the church!

Stephen Brown
Seminary professor, broadcaster
Author of *Talk the Walk: How to be Right Without Being Insufferable.*

Wow! Larry Dixon hits the nail on the head when he chides us Christians (with strong biblical support) about our isolationism and failure to deliberately reach out to and befriend a lost world. I found this book especially credible and helpful because the author doesn't speak from a position of superiority, but as one who himself struggles with sharing his Christian faith with non-believers. While laced with good humor, this deadly serious book is must reading for all followers of Christ.

Dr. George W. Murray
Former President and Chancellor
Columbia International University, Columbia, South Carolina)

Larry Dixon has written a book that is easy to read but strikes at the heart of personal evangelism. He points us to Jesus, the friend of sinners, as a model for bringing others to Christ. Larry backs up his theology of evangelism with personal illustrations and experiences of sharing Christ among his circle of friends over the years. Solidly grounded in biblical truth, his book will inspire you to broaden your circle of friends for the sake of the gospel.

Philip Boom
President, Emmaus Bible College

Dr. Larry Dixon offers challenge, accountability, great exegesis, and practical ideas on how the church can recapture its heart for the Great Commission, one friend at a time. *Unlike Jesus* is a powerful reminder that the church can easily drift toward isolationism in our fear of becoming like "the world." This book would be a great tool for individuals and small groups that want to reawaken their hearts for the lost.

Rev. Dr. Jeff Philpott
Sandhills Community Church

UNLIKE JESUS

LET'S STOP UNFRIENDING THE WORLD

Larry Dixon, Ph.D.

Energion Publications
Gonzalez, Florida
August 2019

i

ISBN: 978-1-63199-703-7
Library of Congress Control Number: 2019909717

Energion Publications
PO Box 841
Gonzalez, FL 32560

energion.com
pubs@energion.com

TABLE OF CONTENTS

FOREWORD

There are a lot of books on evangelism. This book is not like the rest of those books.

Most books on evangelism focus on what to tell people, to get them to believe the gospel, how to argue your position from the Bible, or techniques for convincing people that they should become Christians. Dixon's book instead describes how to live in a way that allows you to enter into the world of non-believers and build long lasting friendships with them as a means to sharing the gospel. Rather than a list of things to say, this book focuses on how to engage, love, be loved, listen, share stories and live the gospel in front of people the same way Jesus attracted people to Himself.

Dixon is an uncharacteristic theologian in that he uses very little theological jargon while at the same time expertly exploring the Bible to demonstrate how Jesus managed to build relationships with "sinners" and win them over to Himself. He describes the types of criticism a Christian will probably receive when living in the world and entering into what may be an uncomfortable world of those who do not know Christ. Dixon wrestles with how to live in the world and how to enjoy the world without falling into the trap of being worldly. Chapters seven and eight give practical step by step advice on the process of engagement.

Dixon is also uncharacteristic of most theologians in that he is very playful and humorous. He believes that non-Christians must see joy and delight in us as an invitation to discuss spiritual matters. His quotes from a wide variety of authors and songwriters is well worth the price of the book.

I have known and taught with Dixon for over a decade. He has the integrity to write this book. He uses tennis, chess, ping pong, meals around the table and dialogue to invite people into relationships with the hope of entering into spiritual discussion and a salvation experience.

If you believe there is a heaven and hell, a loving God who does not want any to perish and are willing to leave the comfort of the Christian bubble to enter into relationships with non-Christians for the sake of the gospel, then this book is for you.

Allan McKechnie
Professor Emeritus
Columbia International University

INTRODUCTION

I've never been unfriended on Facebook. That's probably because I'm a neophyte and am just beginning to spend time with that connection. I know. I know. Technological Neanderthal is the term in your mind right now, correct? But I understand that it must be painful for some to be unfriended or defriended.

Have we who want to follow Christ unfriended the very ones He came to save? As we will see, there is a massive difference between being a "friend of sinners" (which Jesus was, Matthew 11:19) and being a "friend of the world" (which, understood properly, none of us should be, James 4:4).

What draws you to another person? It may be their similar likes and dislikes to yours. It may be their pleasant company or their engaging smile. But what really deeply attracts you to someone else?

True friendship involves "affection, sympathy, empathy, honesty, altruism, mutual understanding and compassion, the enjoyment of each other's company, trust, and the ability to be oneself, express one's feelings, and make mistakes without fear of judgment from the friend. While there is no practical limit on what types of people can form a friendship, friends tend to share common backgrounds, occupations, or interests, and have similar demographics."[1]

Now *that's* a mouthful! For me friendship involves genuine love. You know they love you. You know they care deeply about you. You know they won't forsake you when life gets hard, or circumstances change, or you have a sour day. They stick with you. Through thick or thin. And whether that love is of a more romantic variety or just basic, solid friendship, you are drawn to them like small lead beads are to a powerful magnet. You can't help but want to be around them, to talk with them, or to simply be together. Silent. Breathing the same air. Being in the same room.

Jesus had that impact on the outcasts of His culture. His personality, how He treated others, His words of kindness were

1   https://www.definitions.net/definition/friendship

irresistible. To the downtrodden. The sinners. The prostitutes. The hated IRS agents of the day.

There is no substitution for genuine love. And the Lord Jesus genuinely loved sinners. He came for them. He spent time with them. He sought them out. And He died for them. How dare we do less?

This book will make the case that Jesus was a friend of sinners. His love for them attracted them to Himself and drove the religious windbags away from Him. And though the latter was sad, it did not deter Him from His mission of loving the lost.

We who say we are followers of Jesus fail Him in many ways. Thank God for the chance to repent and allow God the Holy Spirit to change us! If you have so many lost friends that you've lost count, and if each of them knows where you stand spiritually, and they are convinced that you love them with an unconditional love, then go get your money back for this book. This book is not for you.

But if you begin to realize that your life is over-stuffed with Christian friends and Christian meetings and Christian casseroles and Christian missionary stories, and that there is precious little room left for significant relationships with lost people, then I've written this book for you.

I will first prove that Jesus was a friend of sinners. I will then do my best to dismantle and destroy **five excuses** which Jesus-followers give for not loving the lost as He did. Are you listening? Really listening? I'll make the case that we must listen to the stories of our lost friends if we want to develop meaningful relationships with them. I will also seek to remind us of that terrible reality of true lostness — and how we fit in God's rescue mission.

I will deal with the question, what do we have in common with unsaved people? We know that we can be their good friends, but can (should) they be ours?

I'm so sold on this need in my life that I've even surveyed several of my lost friends. We will look at some of their responses and how we might engage them and their questions or accusations.

I actually believe that we should play games with them and be prepared to tell them some good jokes. Really. But we must stop unfriending them first.

CHAPTER ONE:

"What a Friend We Have in Jesus" ♫
(traditional hymn)

"True friendship is when you walk into their house and your WiFi connects automatically." (Author Unknown)

"Friendship is born at that moment when one person says to another: 'What! You too? I thought I was the only one.'" (C.S. Lewis)

"I don't need a friend who changes when I change and who nods when I nod; my shadow does that much better." (Plutarch)

We know that Jesus is our friend. But was He a "friend of sinners"? The text that gives rise to that claim is found in Matthew 11 where we read:

16 "To what can I compare this generation? They are like children sitting in the marketplaces and calling out to others: 17 "'We played the pipe for you, and you did not dance; we sang a dirge, and you did not mourn.' 18 For John came neither eating nor drinking, and they say, 'He has a demon.' 19 The Son of Man came eating and drinking, and they say, 'Here is a glutton and a drunkard, a friend of tax collectors and sinners.' But wisdom is proved right by her deeds."

There is so much in this passage that we must think about. The Lord Jesus is giving His evaluation of His contemporary culture and He says that it is like a bunch of pouting, sulking children! They are ticked, He says, because He and John the Baptist (the "you" of verse 17 is plural) aren't dancing to their tunes. He and John the Baptist are neither rejoicing nor mourning to their music — and they are upset with both of them. Their vocal mockery and taunt-

ing highlight the fact that Jesus is living out His life to the music
of another Musician. And this did not please them.

The Specific Charges

As we think about Matthew 11, we see that Jesus' contemporary culture was acting like preadolescent critics. Jesus' culture
leveled specific charges against both Jesus and John the Baptist.
Neither conformed to the expectations of their culture; neither
John the Baptist nor Jesus danced or mourned on cue. It sounds as
if Jesus might have even mockingly sung those words: "We played
the pipe for you, and you did not dance; we sang a dirge, and you
did not mourn." The culture was miffed because neither lived up
to its expectations.

A Demonic John the Baptist?

Jesus takes their challenge head-on. He says, "For John came
neither eating nor drinking, and they say, 'He has a demon.'" (v.
18). John the Baptist was a strange fellow, was he not? We read
that his "clothes were made of camel's hair, and he had a leather
belt around his waist. His food was locusts and wild honey." (Matthew 3). Unlike expensive camel's hair sport coats today (a Brooks
Brothers camel hair sport jacket goes for $698), John's dress was
basic and simple. His clothes were functional not fashionable. He
would not have graced the cover of the magazine GQ by any stretch
of the imagination. He didn't care about clothing.

And when it came to cuisine, John spent no energy pursuing
fancy food. He scavenged what he could find in nature — locusts
and wild honey. He didn't have a garden. He didn't tend any live-
stock. He lived off the land — and the bugs. His frugal lifestyle
was apparent in both his dress and his diet.

How was John the Baptist regarded by his generation? How
did they view his austere and simple life? They charged him with
being demonized! His laser-like focus on his task of preparing the
way for the Messiah by preaching and baptizing left him no time

for fashion or fancy dining. And his frugality opened him up to the charge that he must have a demon!

An Indulgent Son of God?

Jesus makes it clear that He also was the target of this mocking, childish culture. He states plainly, "The Son of Man came eating and drinking, and they say, 'Here is a glutton and a drunkard . . .'" (v. 19). Jesus was the opposite of John the Baptist in several ways — and He was criticized for His lifestyle.

He is accused of gluttony. Wait a minute! Jesus knew His Old Testament Scriptures. And gluttony was clearly condemned by God. He knew Proverbs 23 which says, "Do not join those who drink too much wine or gorge themselves on meat, for drunkards and gluttons become poor, and drowsiness clothes them in rags." (vv. 20-21). He was certainly acquainted with Proverbs 28:7 which says, "He who keeps the law is a discerning son, but a companion of gluttons disgraces his father." There is even the stern warning in Proverbs 23 which says, "When you sit to dine with a ruler, note well what is before you, and put a knife to your throat if you are given to gluttony." (v. 2).

Although the New Testament was not yet written (and the Holy Spirit would later inspire the Apostle Paul to write, "Do not get drunk on wine, which leads to debauchery. Instead, be filled with the Spirit" [Ephesians 5:18]), Jesus well knew the Old Testament's warnings about overindulgence in drink. He knew Proverbs 20's admonition that "Wine is a mocker and beer a brawler; whoever is led astray by them is not wise" (v. 1). He was well-acquainted with Proverbs 31:4-5 which says, "it is not for kings to drink wine, not for rulers to crave beer, lest they drink and forget what has been decreed, and deprive all the oppressed of their rights." Jesus was neither a priest nor a prophet who staggered from beer or was befuddled with wine (Isaiah 28:7). And He was certainly not one who lingered over wine or asked, "When will I wake up so I can find another drink?" (see Proverbs 23:29-33). He was most definitely not guilty of drunkenness.

We are not to let our appetites control us, but we are to exercise authority over our eating and drinking. (See Deuteronomy 21:20, Proverbs 23:2, 2 Peter 1:5-7, 2 Timothy 3:1-9, and 2 Corinthians 10:5.) The ability to say "no" to anything in excess—self-control—is one of the fruits of the Spirit common to all believers (Galatians 5:22).

Whereas John the Baptist was thought to be demonized because of his austerity, Jesus was accused of being a glutton and a drunkard because of His indulgence. Please don't tell my Baptist friends this, but *Jesus drank wine*! He did. Welch's grape juice had not yet been invented. Jesus drank alcoholic beverages.

You know that the first miracle that the fourth gospel records is Jesus' turning the water into wine at the wedding of Cana, right? Someone has said that the church has been trying to turn that wine back into water ever since!

When I was a young believer, shortly after all the dinosaurs had become extinct, I remember 1 Thessalonians 5:22 often being quoted to me, a teenager, from the King James Bible (of course): "Abstain from all appearance of evil." The point being driven home to me (I think) was that Jesus-followers shouldn't be seen in bars or roller skating rinks or movie theaters.

Did *Jesus* abstain from all appearance of evil? Apparently not, for His eating and drinking opened Him up to the charges of being a glutton and a drunkard. It was only years later, after I got a bit of New Testament Greek under my belt, that I learned a critical truth. The word "appearance" in the King James' translation of that verse literally means "form" or "kind." We are to abstain from every form or kind of evil. Eating and drinking are not evil in themselves, but become evil when one over-indulges.

If the Lord Jesus is our model, then we *should* be eating and drinking with sinners! Let's not get sidetracked by the alcohol issue (I'm pretty much a tea-totaler having worked in a detox hospital for alcoholics). The *point* is that Jesus was social, He spent time with sinners, and He was criticized for His habit of hanging around the lost!

"Jesus, How Do You Plead?"

If there had been a trial of Jesus on these three issues, I believe He would have taken the stand in defense of Himself. To the charge of being a glutton, He would have said, "Not guilty! I have never over-indulged in food." To the charge of being a drunkard, He would have said, "Not guilty! I have never gotten drunk!" But to the charge of being a friend of tax collectors and sinners, He would have said, "GUILTY! GUILTY! GUILTY! That's the kind of people I came to save!"

A Friend of Tax Collectors and Sinners

My wife and I try to be honest in paying our taxes. Because we have a small Amazon book business, we have to work very hard to account for all our purchases, itemize our expenses, and report our earnings. I'm sure our work is imperfect. If we had an IRS agent living in our neighborhood, I'm fairly certain we wouldn't seek to be best friends with him or her.

Jesus was a "friend of tax collectors and sinners." Tax collectors were Jews who were working for the Roman government to collect a 1% tax on a person's income. That may not seem like much, but tax collectors were allowed to charge over and above that amount and pocket the rest. Considered traitors, they were shunned by self-respecting Jewish society. Jesus went out of His way to draft a tax collector as one of His disciples!

One IRS Agent Is Drafted and Another Treed

The description of Jesus' selecting a tax collector as one of His disciples is given to us in Matthew 9. There we read,

> 9 As Jesus went on from there, he saw a man named Matthew sitting at the tax collector's booth. "Follow me," he told him, and Matthew got up and followed him. 10 While Jesus was having dinner at Matthew's house, many tax collectors and sinners came and ate with him and his disciples. 11 When the Pharisees saw this, they asked his disciples,

"Why does your teacher eat with tax collectors and sinners?"
12 On hearing this, Jesus said, "It is not the healthy who need
a doctor, but the sick. 13 But go and learn what this means:
'I desire mercy, not sacrifice.' For I have not come to call the
righteous, but sinners."

Notice that Jesus has dinner at Matthew's house. And "many"
tax collectors and sinners came and ate with Him and His disciples.
Jesus spent time with those two groups. And He gets criticized for
it.

Jesus' disciples are grilled on why Jesus ate with tax collectors
and sinners. Jesus overhears their question and responds, "It is not
the healthy who need a doctor, but the sick. . . . I have not come
to call the righteous, but sinners" (v. 13).

On another occasion we learn of Jesus' passing through Jericho
and meeting a chief tax-collector by the name of Zacchaeus (Luke
19). But Zac had a problem. A problem not solved by the wealth he
obtained collecting taxes. He was short. He wanted to see Jesus, but
his geographical disability would not let him see over the crowd.
Then he thought back to his childhood and a brilliant idea came to
him: "I can still climb trees, can't I?" And that's exactly what he did.

He ran ahead of the Jesus procession, found a sycamore-fig
tree, and shimmied up! Zac's plan was that he would see Jesus. He
didn't realize that Jesus would look up and see him. And would
call him by name.

Jesus looked up and said, "Zacchaeus, come down immediately. I must stay at your house today." (v. 5). We read that Zac came
down immediately and welcomed Jesus into his home.

The text tells us that "All the people saw this and began to
mutter, 'He has gone to be the guest of a sinner.'" (v. 7). They don't
even refer to Zac by name. He is simply categorized as "a sinner."

Zac declared to the Lord, "Look, Lord! Here and now I give
half of my possessions to the poor, and if I have cheated anybody
out of anything, I will pay back four times the amount." (v. 8). For
a chief tax collector, this was genuine repentance! It does not seem

that Zac is referring to a past action, but making a promise on the spot to do what was right.

Jesus' response to Zac is quite telling, for He declares that "salvation has come to this house, because this man, too, is a son of Abraham." (v. 9). Jesus is not saying that Zac has purchased salvation with his promises of financial generosity to the poor. Even though in the minds of Jewish culture Zac was a traitor to his own people, in Jesus' opinion he was still a son of Abraham and one for whom Jesus came. Jesus then declares, "For the Son of Man came to seek and to save the lost." (v. 10). And as a friend of tax-collectors, Jesus sought out the short Zac and saved him.

The Poor Examples of Tax Collectors and Pagans

We also see that Jesus repeated the common belief that the tax collectors and pagans were looked down upon by well-respecting Jewish culture. In Matthew 5 Jesus says, "46 If you love those who love you, what reward will you get? Are not even the tax collectors doing that? 47 And if you greet only your own people, what are you doing more than others? Do not even pagans do that? 48 Be perfect, therefore, as your heavenly Father is perfect." Jesus is saying that even tax collectors were known to love those who loved them! And pagans had the reputation for greeting only their own people.

A Tax-Collector Commended

In fact, Jesus tells a famous parable that features a tax collector! We read in Luke 18:

> 9 To some who were confident of their own righteousness and looked down on everyone else, Jesus told this parable: 10 "Two men went up to the temple to pray, one a Pharisee and the other a tax collector. 11 The Pharisee stood by himself and prayed: 'God, I thank you that I am not like other people—robbers, evildoers, adulterers—or even like this tax collector. 12 I fast twice a week and give a tenth of all I get.' 13 "But the tax collector stood at a distance. He would not even look up to heaven, but beat his breast and said, 'God,

have mercy on me, a sinner.' 14 "I tell you that this man, rather than the other, went home justified before God. For all those who exalt themselves will be humbled, and those who humble themselves will be exalted."

It's not the self-righteous Pharisee who comes out as the example in this parable. The one to be admired is none other than "this tax collector."

Jesus did not come to call the righteous, but sinners to repentance (Luke 5:32). And that's precisely what the tax collector does in Luke 18. He repents. "God, have mercy on me, a sinner" (v. 13). Then Jesus authoritatively declares, "[T]his man, rather than the other, went home justified before God." (v. 14). As God manifest in the flesh, Jesus could categorically declare that this man had found forgiveness with God.

"Treat Them as You Would a Pagan or a Tax Collector"

There is one other text where Jesus refers to tax collectors and pagans (or sinners). We read in Matthew 18 how we should treat a brother who sins (and refuses to repent):

> 15 "If your brother or sister sins, go and point out their fault, just between the two of you. If they listen to you, you have won them over. 16 But if they will not listen, take one or two others along, so that 'every matter may be established by the testimony of two or three witnesses.' 17 If they still refuse to listen, tell it to the church; and if they refuse to listen even to the church, treat them as you would a pagan or a tax collector."

In this critical text about church discipline, Jesus deals with the sad possibility that the one sinning might refuse to repent and be restored to the church and the Lord. If that person rejects the counsel of the church, Jesus says, "treat them as you would a pagan or a tax collector" (v. 17).

But we must ask the question — how did *Jesus* treat tax collectors and pagans? He sought to win them to salvation! He came for them. He ate with them and was criticized for spending time with them. This text in Matthew 18 is not saying that we should shun such individuals. It is saying that we should treat them as lost people if they are behaving like lost people behave.[2]

Jesus — The Seeker of the Lost

Jesus was a friend of tax collectors and sinners. He came to seek the lost. He did not come for the self-righteous, but for sinners. He had dinner with a tax collector (Matthew) and many other tax collectors and sinners ate with Him and His disciples (Matthew 9:10). The Pharisees ask His disciples why He ate with tax collectors and sinners (Matthew 9:11). Jesus responds, "I have not come to call the righteous, but sinners." (Matthew 9:13).

Mark, in recording Jesus' eating with the tax collector Matthew (Mark calls him "Levi" in his account), says that "there were many [tax collectors and sinners] who followed [Jesus]" (Mark 2:15). Mark records Jesus' answer to the teachers of the law who were questioning His eating with these two groups: "It is not the healthy who need a doctor, but the sick. I have not come to call the righteous, but sinners." (Mark 2:17).

Luke records the same event — the complaint of the Pharisees and the teachers of the law about Jesus' eating with these two groups — and says that Jesus responded, "I have not come to call the righteous, but sinners to repentance." (Luke 5:32).

This eating with tax collectors and sinners was such an important practice of the Lord Jesus that all three synoptic gospels record it. How is it possible that we have missed this central habit of our Savior? If He is our example in every area of life, then a significant portion of the people we hang out with ought to be tax collectors and sinners!

---

2   See our later discussion in the next chapter that says we should "shun" habitually-sinning believers. Shunning probably means that we should not financially support such believers, rather than ever having a meal with them.

I understand a retired pastor of a growing church, who is passionate to reach "people far from God," occasionally challenged his church staff to "stand to your feet and give the first names of three unsaved friends you are trying to reach for the Lord. Ready? Go!" Could you stand to your feet and provide three names? If not, could it be said that, in this area, you are clearly unlike Jesus?

The preacher Vance Havner said, "An excuse is the skin of a reason stuffed with a lie." We want to analyze and dismantle the five excuses we give for being unlike Jesus in this area in our next few chapters.

QUESTIONS FOR CHAPTER ONE:

1. Jesus says that His generation was mad at both Him and John the Baptist. With what did they charge John the Baptist? Why?

2. What were the charges against Jesus by His generation? If He were in a court of law, how might He respond to each charge?

3. How did Jesus treat tax collectors and sinners/pagans? How should we treat a professing Christian who refuses to repent of his or her sin? How have you been treated by the church?

4. How does one know when to be frugal and when to indulge? What guidance do you get from looking at the life and mission of both John the Baptist and the Lord Jesus?

CHAPTER TWO:

"It's a Small World After All . . ." ♬
(Disney theme song)

"Nothing exposes religion more to the reproach of its enemies than the worldliness and hard-heartedness of its professors." (Matthew Henry)

"It is not this earth, nor the men who inhabit it, nor the sphere of our legitimate activity, that we may not love; but the way in which the love is given, which constitutes worldliness." (Frederick W. Robertson)

"You and I have need of the strongest spell that can be found to wake us from the evil enchantment of worldliness." (C.S. Lewis)

"Prosperity knits a man to the World. He feels that he is 'finding his place in it', while really it is finding its place in him." (C.S. Lewis, *Screwtape Letters*)

What in the world is the Christian anyway? How is the Jesus-follower to relate to this culture that is often so anti-God?

When I was a young believer, back in the days of Ben Franklin and his experiments with his kite and lightning, my spiritual mentors were certain about one area that impacted my teenaged life — worldliness. They were convinced that roller skating was dancing on wheels, that cosmetics for young women were of the devil, and that the Beatles were each, in turn, the Antichrist.

Beards were worldly. I had to shave my beard when I came home from the mission field on a brief furlough just to give a ministry update to my home church. The music of the Rolling Stones and the Monkees and the Dave Clark Five were all of the Evil One. Interesting that Frank Sinatra's songs were played on record players in elders' homes ("Not as one on bended knee . . . I did it

my way!"). Not being "worldly" meant not spending time with
lost people, unless one were inviting them to a church meeting.

What in the World Is Worldliness?

There's a lot of confusion about worldliness. Garrison Keil-
lor (who grew up in a conservative Christian home) said he was
taught that playing cards was okay as long as one didn't play with
a full deck! Older believers in my home church were certain what
worldliness was. And in their concern for us young people, we were
warned time and again about conforming to this world.

Reflecting back on those growing up years, there is much for
which I am thankful in that church. However, child abuse and
racism were also present — and I don't remember a single sermon
or lecture on such issues. Social issues were of the world — which
meant we were not to get involved.

The basic advice — either given privately or publicly from the
pulpit — was we have to avoid becoming like the world. And most
of us understood that as isolation from sinners, spending all our free
time in church meetings, and eating casseroles. I don't remember
even one sermon about Matthew 11 and becoming a "friend of
sinners" like Jesus was.

Worldliness was and is far more than the music one listens
to, the places one frequents, or the friends one has. Worldliness is
a spirit, an attitude that says, in the words of the great theologian
Billy Joel, "This is my life. Leave me alone!"[3]

---

3   John Piper gives a good description of worldliness: "I am wired by nature
      to love the same toys that the world loves. I start to fit in. I start to love
      what others love. I start to call earth 'home.' Before you know it, I am
      calling luxuries 'needs' and using my money just the way unbelievers do.
      I begin to forget the war. I don't think much about people perishing.
      Missions and unreached people drop out of my mind. I stop dreaming
      about the triumphs of grace. I sink into a secular mind-set that looks
      first to what man can do, not what God can do. It is a terrible sickness.
      And I thank God for those who have forced me again and again toward a
      wartime mind-set." (John Piper, *Don't Waste Your Life*)

Jesus Prays for . . . Us!

I have recently examined Jesus' high priestly prayer found in John 17 and have discovered what He thought about "the world." Defining "the world" is not an easy task, by the way. The same biblical writer John who says in John 3:16 that God "so loved the world" also says (in I John 2:15) that we "are not to love the world." What gives? He loved the world but we aren't supposed to? I thought He was our model.

The answer, of course, is that the expression "the world" (cosmos) can have several different meanings. "The world" can mean the planet, the people of the planet, or the pagan system opposing God and the things of God. God so loved the world of people in John 3:16. We are not to love the system that opposes God and the things of God in I John 2:15.

But the key passage that helps regarding the believer's "place" in the world is John 17. Here's what the Lord prays there:

> After Jesus said this, he looked toward heaven and prayed: "Father, the hour has come. Glorify your Son, that your Son may glorify you. 2 For you granted him authority over all people that he might give eternal life to all those you have given him. 3 Now this is eternal life: that they know you, the only true God, and Jesus Christ, whom you have sent. 4 I have brought you glory on earth by finishing the work you gave me to do. 5 And now, Father, glorify me in your presence with the glory I had with you before the world began.
>
> Jesus Prays for His Disciples
>
> 6 "I have revealed you to those whom you gave me out of the world. They were yours; you gave them to me and they have obeyed your word. 7 Now they know that everything you have given me comes from you. 8 For I gave them the words you gave me and they accepted them. They knew with certainty that I came from you, and they believed that you sent me. 9 I pray for them. I am not praying for the world, but for those you have given me, for they are yours. 10 All I

have is yours, and all you have is mine. And glory has come to me through them. 11 I will remain in the world no longer, but they are still in the world, and I am coming to you. Holy Father, protect them by the power of your name, the name you gave me, so that they may be one as we are one. 12 While I was with them, I protected them and kept them safe by that name you gave me. None has been lost except the one doomed to destruction so that Scripture would be fulfilled. 13 "I am coming to you now, but I say these things while I am still in the world, so that they may have the full measure of my joy within them. 14 I have given them your word and the world has hated them, for they are not of the world any more than I am of the world. 15 My prayer is not that you take them out of the world but that you protect them from the evil one. 16 They are not of the world, even as I am not of it. 17 Sanctify them by the truth; your word is truth. 18 As you sent me into the world, I have sent them into the world. 19 For them I sanctify myself, that they too may be truly sanctified. 20 "My prayer is not for them alone. I pray also for those who will believe in me through their message, 21 that all of them may be one, Father, just as you are in me and I am in you. May they also be in us so that the world may believe that you have sent me. 22 I have given them the glory that you gave me, that they may be one as we are one— 23 I in them and you in me—so that they may be brought to complete unity. Then the world will know that you sent me and have loved them even as you have loved me. 24 "Father, I want those you have given me to be with me where I am, and to see my glory, the glory you have given me because you loved me before the creation of the world. 25 "Righteous Father, though the world does not know you, I know you, and they know that you have sent me. 26 I have made you known to them, and will continue to make you known in order that the love you have for me may be in them and that I myself may be in them."

There is so much in this passage that we must examine. The Lord Jesus uses the word cosmos seventeen times here in John 17.

Sometimes the word means the planet, sometimes the people of the planet, and sometimes the pagan system opposing God and the things of God.

If we go through each use of that term cosmos and substitute one of those three meanings, we might learn a bit about our place in the world.

Here is my best translation of those verses in John 17 in which Jesus uses the word cosmos (substituting one of our three definitions for the general word "world"):

> "And now, Father, glorify me in your presence with the glory I had with you before **the planet** began." (v. 5). … I have revealed you to those whom you gave me out of **the pagan system**. (v. 6). … I pray for them, I am not praying for **the people of the planet**, but for those you have given me, for they are yours. (v. 9). … I will remain in **the planet** no longer, but they are still in **the planet**, and I am coming to you. (vv. 10-11). … I am coming to you now, but I say these things while I am still in **the planet**, so that they may have the full measure of my joy within them. (v. 13). … I have given them your word and **the pagan system** has hated them, for they are not of **the pagan system** any more than I am of **the pagan system**. (v. 14). … My prayer is not that you take them out of **the planet** but that you protect them from the evil one." (v. 15). … They are not of **the pagan system**, even as I am not of it. (v. 16). … As you sent me into **the people of the planet**, I have sent them into **the people of the planet**. (v. 18). … My prayer is not for them alone. I pray also for those who will believe in me through their message, that all of them may be one, Father, just as you are in me and I am in you. May they also be in us so that **the people of the planet** may believe the you have sent me. (vv. 20-21). … I in them and you in me — so that they may be brought to complete unity. Then **the people of the planet** will know that you have sent me and have loved them even as you have loved me." (v. 23). … Father, I want those you have given me to be with me where I am, and to see my glory, the glory you have given me because you loved me before the creation of **the planet**. (v. 24). … Righteous Father, though

the people of the planet do not know you, I know you, and they know that you have sent me." (v. 25).

There are ten conclusions that we can draw from looking at John 17 in this way:

1. The full deity of the Lord Jesus is foundational. He had the Father's glory before creation (v. 5) and was loved by the Father before the creation came into existence (v. 24).

2. We all are in the pagan system opposing God until He saves us. No one is spiritually neutral. We are all enemies of God before conversion (v. 6).

3. Jesus personally prays for each of us (v. 9).

4. He is leaving the planet, but we are staying here (vv. 10-11).

5. He says these things while here on the planet so that we might have the full measure of His joy. Now. Here. (v. 13).

6. We should not be surprised that the pagan system hates us, for it hated Him! (v. 14).

7. Jesus prays for our protection not our escape from this planet (v. 15).

8. We have been sent/commissioned by the Lord Jesus to the people of this planet (v. 18).

9. The unity of Jesus-followers can lead the people of the planet to belief in Him (vv. 20-23).

10. The people of the planet do not know the Father, but Jesus does (v. 25).

Thank God for His rescuing us out of "the world"! But there is no hint of a kind of evacuation theology here. We are not to be simply standing around waiting to be raptured (as glorious as that future event will be). We are to be on mission right where we are. On this planet.

But we have enemies — and the pagan system (inspired by the Evil One, Satan) will use every tactic to instill in us the priorities and values of a God-less system. And for that challenge we need protection from the Lord Jesus.

The Wrong Enemy?

However, we must think carefully here. It is not the world itself (the planet) that is the Christian's adversary. As we saw from Robertson's quote, "It is not this earth, nor the men who inhabit it, nor the sphere of our legitimate activity, that we may not love; but the way in which the love is given, which constitutes worldliness."

In his excellent book *Becoming Worldly Saints: Can You Serve Jesus and Still Enjoy Your Life?*, Michael Wittmer makes some strong points about the believer's relationship to "the world."

We have often been taught that this world is nothing more than "the waiting room of heaven." In fact, the way we Christians often look at the Christian life and the world can turn us into "stodgy, droopy, hermit Christians." We are to be both world-affirming (after all, God created this world) and world-denying (we are not to find our ultimate happiness in the things of this world). Wittmer says, "God doesn't want us to feel false guilt for enjoying the good world God has given us. The truth of eternity doesn't obliterate our earthly experiences; it infuses them with heavenly significance."

Can we talk? Would we be surprised if our non-Christian friends said to us, "If I choose to follow Jesus, according to Christians I'll really have to deny God's good creation, right?" Wittmer writes, "Being a Christian must not become an obstacle to being human." In fact, he rightly points out that if we want to attract people to Jesus, our lives must be attractive.

Because everything matters in this life, we are to do our best work. Colossians 3 says, "Whatever you do, work at it with all your heart, as working for the Lord, not for human masters, since you know that you will receive an inheritance from the Lord as a reward." Rather than pursue a kind of escapist theology, we should live our lives to the glory of God here. "We are earthlings," Wittmer says, "for heaven's sake!"

Colossians 3 says that it is the sins of the world that we are to avoid. Wittmer writes, "As humans we should be comfortable with the *things* of this world. God created us to breathe oxygen, eat food, and contribute to the overall health of the planet. As Christians we must oppose the *bad actions* of this world. It's the sin of this world — not its stuff — that should drive us nuts." (57). The truth is that when read correctly, we won't find one negative word about creation in all of the Scriptures.

Be a Blessing — Here!

We are to cultivate the earth, using our gifts to be the blessing of God "to that slice of creation that lies within our influence!" We are to have a sense of vocation or calling that encourages us to make a difference. In this world.

This world is not our permanent home. It will be replaced by the New Heavens and the New Earth (Isaiah 65-66). But it is to be cared for, enjoyed, and used for the glory of the Creator, even though it is broken. "If you enjoy being human," Wittmer writes, "and you enjoy being here, you are going to love the New Earth."

So, if I want to be a friend of sinners like Jesus, I have to live in this world without the worldly system taking up residence in me. I can enjoy the good things the Lord has created without falling into a worship of creation.[4] I cannot use the excuse that in order not to be a friend of the world I must isolate myself from its inhabitants. "Worldliness" must be defined biblically, recognized in its present cultural manifestations, and denounced as being anti-God. If I want to be a friend of sinners, like Jesus was.

Friend of the World?

There are two other texts that we must look at when considering worldliness. We read in James 4 —

---

4   David Kinnaman puts it this way: "Being salt and light demands two things: we practice purity in the midst of a fallen world and yet we live in proximity to this fallen world. If you don't hold up both truths in tension, you invariably become useless and separated from the world God loves." (David Kinnaman, *unChristian: What a New Generation Really Thinks about Christianity... and Why It Matters*)

What causes fights and quarrels among you? Don't they come from your desires that battle within you? 2 You desire but do not have, so you kill. You covet but you cannot get what you want, so you quarrel and fight. You do not have because you do not ask God. 3 When you ask, you do not receive, because you ask with wrong motives, that you may spend what you get on your pleasures.4 You adulterous people, don't you know that friendship with the world means enmity against God? Therefore, anyone who chooses to be a friend of the world becomes an enemy of God. 5 Or do you think Scripture says without reason that he jealously longs for the spirit he has caused to dwell in us? 6 But he gives us more grace. That is why Scripture says: "God opposes the proud but shows favor to the humble." 7 Submit yourselves, then, to God. Resist the devil, and he will flee from you. 8 Come near to God and he will come near to you. Wash your hands, you sinners, and purify your hearts, you double-minded. 9 Grieve, mourn and wail. Change your laughter to mourning and your joy to gloom. 10 Humble yourselves before the Lord, and he will lift you up. 11 Brothers and sisters, do not slander one another. Anyone who speaks against a brother or sister or judges them speaks against the law and judges it. When you judge the law, you are not keeping it, but sitting in judgment on it. 12 There is only one Lawgiver and Judge, the one who is able to save and destroy. But you—who are you to judge your neighbor?

In this fascinating passage, we have a discussion of all three enemies of the believer: the world, the flesh, and the devil. The text first deals with our "flesh" (a term that can simply mean our bodies, as in Ephesians 5:29 ["no one ever hated their own body"] or it can refer to our sinful nature, as in Rom. 8 ["the flesh desires what is contrary to the Spirit"]).

James discusses our sinful nature in verses 1-3 of this text. We have desires inside us that are at war with God (v. 1). Those desires lead to killing, coveting, quarreling, and fighting (v. 2). Those same desires even impact our prayer lives, causing us to ask with wrong motives or to simply pursue our desired pleasures (v. 3).

James then discusses the world in verses 4-6. But let's first observe what he says about the devil in verses 7-10. There we learn that we are to submit to God, to resist the devil, and to humble ourselves before the Lord.

But what about the world? We see in verses 4-6 that we have adulterous hearts that cause us to become spiritually unfaithful to the Lord (v. 4). Loving the world system that opposes God and the things of God is precisely the "friendship with the world" that James condemns. The choice is simple: choosing to be a friend of the world means becoming an enemy of God (v. 4). And such spiritual promiscuity grieves God's heart which jealously wants to guard our relationship with Him (v. 5).

But being a friend of sinners like the Lord Jesus is not the same as being a friend of the world. We are to love the people of the world, cherish God's good creation of the world, but recognize and turn away from the principles of the world that are anti-God.

Worldliness, defined biblically, is a serious threat to the believer. But we are to be friends, not of the world, but of the people for whom Jesus came. Is isolation from sinners a less risky course? Absolutely. But that choice, while comforting and easier for us, is not the path laid out for us by our Savior.

Two Catastrophic Conclusions

The last passage we want to consider to counter the excuse of a fear of worldliness is I Corinthians 5. There we read:

> 9 I wrote to you in my letter not to associate with sexually immoral people— 10 not at all meaning the people of this world who are immoral, or the greedy and swindlers, or idolaters. In that case you would have to leave this world. 11 But now I am writing to you that you must not associate with anyone who claims to be a brother or sister but is sexually immoral or greedy, an idolater or slanderer, a drunkard or swindler. Do not even eat with such people. 12 What business is it of mine to judge those outside the

church? Are you not to judge those inside? 13 God will judge those outside. "Expel the wicked person from among you."

The Corinthian Christians had a lot of problems, didn't they? They were actually boasting about a man who was sleeping with his step-mother! I have a step-mother, but . . . Yuck!

Those believers needed to be corrected on many issues, but this one was particularly troublesome. And as the Apostle Paul writes them to bring that sinning member into a state of repentance and restoration, he realizes that they had seriously misunderstood his God-inspired instructions.

Ruining Evangelism

Paul advised these believers "not to associate with sexually immoral people" (v. 9). But he didn't mean "the people of this world." Sins of all sorts are rampant among "the people of this world." And Paul lists some of those sins: immorality, greed, swindling, idolatry. One does not need to look far to find "sinners." But those are not the people from whom Paul is advocating isolation. In fact, the very idea of isolating oneself from sinners is ridiculous, for as Paul says, "in that case you would have to leave this world" (v. 10).

I can hear some Christians (myself included) saying, "Great! I didn't like this sin-infested planet anyway! Let's buy ascension robes, climb the highest mountain near us, and wait for the rapture! *We're out of here!*" But that's not what Paul meant. Isolation from sinners ruins evangelism (it's hard to evangelize those with whom we have no contact).

Destroying Discipleship

Paul corrects their misunderstanding by saying that he was referring to anyone "who claims to be a brother or sister but is sexually immoral," etc. He is talking about those who profess faith in Christ but are caught in a habitual sin like immorality, greed, idolatry, slander, drunkenness, or swindling. When we tolerate such on-going sinful behavior by those who claim to be followers of Jesus, we ruin discipleship! And those who practice such sins — and refuse to repent of them and be restored to God and His people — are to be shunned: "Do not even eat with such people" (v. 11).

By their misunderstanding the Corinthians had ruined two major aspects of the Christian life: evangelism and discipleship. They were isolating themselves from the wrong group and they were tolerating the sinful behavior of another wrong group! Toleration of habitual sin by believers destroys discipleship.

Being in the World

We are to be in the world, but the world is not to be in us. Jesus' example of indulging in social situations challenges us to spend significant time with those who are sick and need the Great Physician. James' admonition not to be a friend of the world does not contradict Jesus' being a friend of sinners. And properly defining "the world" is critical to the believer's place in it. We can easily ruin two major aspects of the Christian life (winning the lost and restoring erring brothers and sisters) by isolating ourselves from the wrong group and tolerating the sin of a different wrong group.

When it comes to the behavior of those not yet in God's family, we believers are not in the behavior modification business. It is not our job to get our non-Christian friends to stop cussing, or drinking, or blaspheming, or cavorting, or gossiping, or . . . whatever. In fact, if we make it our mission to clean up the behavior of those not yet in God's family, we are very well making two serious mistakes. The first is we may be perverting the gospel. Really! We might be communicating, "Clean up your life and God will love you." Or "Stop your bad habits and you'll make it to heaven." We are not in the behavior modification business for unbelievers.

The second mistake we are making concerns our own comfort zones. The ungodly language and behavior of lost people makes us uncomfortable. And how easy it is to do everything in our power to increase our own comfort.

But godly discomfort — tolerating the sin of unbelievers and isolating ourselves from unrepentant believers — awaits us. Unless we want to bail out of this world for which Christ died.

Questions for Chapter Two:

1. How would you define worldliness biblically?

2. What one principle about living in this world challenges you the most from our study of John 17?

3. We all long for the Lord Jesus to return for us. But how do we avoid a kind of evacuation theology that keeps us from developing relationships with unbelievers?

4. How can we be friends of sinners and yet not be friends of the world?

5. What two errors did the Corinthians fall into in I Corinthians 5?

Chapter Three:

"I Haven't Got Time for the ..." ♬

(Carly Simon)

"We say we waste time, but that is impossible. We waste ourselves." (Alice Bloch)

"The only reason for time is so that everything doesn't happen at once." (Albert Einstein)

"The greatest gift you can give someone is your time. Because when you give your time, you are giving a portion of your life that you will never get back." (anonymous)

Jesus spent time with sinners. And tax collectors. And even Pharisees. We read in Luke 7 about His spending time with Simon the Pharisee. Let's notice that text:

36 One of the Pharisees asked him to eat with him, and he went into the Pharisee's house and reclined at table. 37 And behold, a woman of the city, who was a sinner, when she learned that he was reclining at table in the Pharisee's house, brought an alabaster flask of ointment, 38 and standing behind him at his feet, weeping, she began to wet his feet with her tears and wiped them with the hair of her head and kissed his feet and anointed them with the ointment. 39 Now when the Pharisee who had invited him saw this, he said to himself, "If this man were a prophet, he would have known who and what sort of woman this is who is touching him, for she is a sinner." 40 And Jesus answering said to him, "Simon, I have something to say to you." And he answered, "Say it, Teacher." 41 "A certain moneylender had two debtors. One owed five hundred denarii, and the other fifty. 42 When they could not pay, he canceled the debt of both. Now which of them will love him more?" 43 Simon answered, "The one, I suppose, for whom he canceled the larger debt." And he said to him, "You have judged rightly." 44 Then turning toward the woman he said to Simon, "Do you see this woman? I entered your house;

you gave me no water for my feet, but she has wet my feet with her tears and wiped them with her hair. 45 You gave me no kiss, but from the time I came in she has not ceased to kiss my feet. 46 You did not anoint my head with oil, but she has anointed my feet with ointment. 47 Therefore I tell you, her sins, which are many, are forgiven—for she loved much. But he who is forgiven little, loves little." 48 And he said to her, "Your sins are forgiven." 49 Then those who were at table with him began to say among themselves, "Who is this, who even forgives sins?" 50 And he said to the woman, "Your faith has saved you; go in peace."

Spending Time with the Super-Religious

This is a fascinating passage. Jesus actually spent time with super-religious people. He didn't avoid them. He did, however, argue with them. Often. But here He is invited to a meal with this Pharisee Simon.

Jesus made Himself comfortable as He "reclined at table" (v. 36). We're not told what Simon's motives were for inviting Jesus to his home, but there Jesus is. Ready to enjoy a meal.

However, there's a dinner-crasher who invites *herself* into that home. This unnamed woman, "a woman of the city," Luke tells us, was "a sinner." She hears of Jesus' presence in Simon's home and comes prepared to repent. She brings an alabaster flask of ointment, stands behind Jesus at His feet, and begins to weep, wetting His feet with her tears and wiping His feet dry with her hair. She then kisses His feet and anoints them with the ointment. She is aware of only one Person in that room — the Lord.

Jesus the Mind-Reader

But this was Simon the Pharisee's home! And he cannot remain silent. Well, he does remain silent, but he thinks a certain thought, more than likely unaware that Jesus could read his mind! He says to himself, "If this man were a prophet, he would have known who and what sort of woman this is who is touching him, for she is a sinner." (v. 39).

Jesus knows what Simon is thinking, so He says, "Simon, I have something to say to you" (v. 40). I wonder if Simon thought to himself, "Did I say what I just thought *out loud*?!"

Jesus then tells a story, a story that is ingenious in its direct application to the present situation — and to Simon's concern. The story is succinct — only 20 words in the Greek language — before Jesus asks Simon a critical question. Two men owed a debtor money. One owed 500 denarii and the other 50. Matthew 20 suggests that one *denarius* was a day's wages. So one debtor owed the moneylender the equivalent of fifty days' wages; the other the equivalent of over five hundred days' wages! But neither could pay off their debt. Both could have been put in jail. Both could have been forced to become indentured servants. But the moneylender "canceled the debt of both" (v. 42). What a gracious moneylender! He was under no obligation to take this action. But he did.

Jesus' piercing question to Simon was straightforward: "Now which of them will love him more?" (v. 42). Simon is trapped by Jesus' logic and has to respond, "The one, I suppose, for whom he canceled the larger debt." (v. 43).

"Do You See This Woman?"

Jesus compliments Simon on his correct answer. And then goes for his heart. Jesus doesn't exactly ream Simon out, but He does dismantle Simon's objection to what is happening in his home. Jesus first asks, "Do you see this woman?" What an interesting question. Of course, he "saw" this woman. He saw her as a sinner, as a "woman of the city." But did he see her as Jesus saw her? Obviously not.

Jesus then states several facts. "I entered your house. You didn't give me water for my feet." Simon had failed to show basic hospitality to Jesus. Jesus then says, "But this woman has done what you should have done. If fact, she has wet my feet with her tears and wiped them with her hair." Jesus continues, "You gave me no kiss. But her kisses of my feet have been continuous since I came into your home." He then states, "You didn't anoint my head with oil, but she has anointed my feet with ointment."

Simon had failed to express simple Middle Eastern hospitality. She used the occasion to do those duties and much more.

Jesus' conclusion is quite dramatic. "Therefore, I tell you, her sins, which are many, are forgiven — for she loved much. But he who is forgiven little, loves little." (v. 47).

The Lord then turns to the woman and says, "Your sins are forgiven." (v. 48). Something that only God can do, Jesus does! No wonder the other dinner guests say among themselves, "Who is this, who even forgives sins?" (v. 49). Jesus then dismisses her with the words, "Your faith has saved you; go in peace." (v. 50).

Religious People Need Forgiveness Too

When we think about spending time with sinners, let's not forget the very religious among us! They are sinners too. They are in need of forgiveness. They need to be shown their sinnership. And that takes *time*.

I try to avoid really religious people. I don't mean brothers and sisters in Christ who are growing in a vital relationship with Him and are seeking to serve Him. I mean the religious zealots among us who stand ready to slap a "HELLO- I'M A SINNER!" name badge on the chest of somebody else. These folk love their certainties and look for others upon whom they can inflict their absolute dogmas. I'm not speaking about the essentials of the faith, but about those many areas where believers are free to disagree with one another.

And their distinctive areas of belief have been elevated to the level of essentials which every sincere Jesus-follower must adopt, they think. Simon had such an opinion. "Does He know what she is? She is a sinner!"

Simon's Oughtness

In fact, Simon's logic is quite strong. He reasoned, if Jesus is a prophet [premise A], he would know what sort of woman this is [premise B], and he would avoid her like the plague [conclusion]. Granting Simon's unarticulated definition of a prophet, his logic was air-tight. Simon no doubt thought that Jesus should have jumped up in horror, grabbed the woman's arm, and publicly scolded her for such outrageous behavior. He should have said to her, "Do you know who I am? How dare you touch me?!" He should have then unceremoniously escorted her out the door. That seems to be what Simon thought Jesus ought to have done.

But Jesus never submits to another person's "oughtness." Instead, He sits there, passively, allowing her to express her love and repentance before this shocked dinner party.

What was wrong with Simon's logic? He reasoned, "If Jesus is a prophet" [premise A] . . . But Jesus indeed was a prophet, a mouthpiece of God. Simon continues: "He would know what sort of woman this is" [premise B] . . . And Jesus knew what sort of woman this was (He says in verse 47, "Therefore, I tell you, her sins, which are many, are forgiven . . ."). "And," Simon reasons, "He would avoid her like the plague" [conclusion]. No, Jesus came for sinners. And avoidance was not His modus operandi.

There was nothing wrong with Simon's logic. The problem was how he defined "prophet" and how he thought "sinners" ought to be treated.

Religious people have settled opinions that need to be challenged. For their definitions and logical syllogisms are not innocuous — they lead people away from the gospel! Just like the Pharisees in John 9 who said of the man born blind, "You were steeped in sin at birth. How dare you lecture us?", Simon the Pharisee branded others as sinners. Which we all are.

God could correct their poor positions by sending an angel with a flaming sword, but His usual way is to enlist His people on such a mission. And missions require time. Jesus spends time with lost *religious* people so they will begin to understand forgiveness and grace.

Twenty-Four Hours, Right?

Although there are a number of other excuses we Christians give for not spending time with sinners, this issue of time cannot be avoided. All of us have exactly 24 hours each day, right? Well, one scientifically-minded person wrote the following question to a website: "Why do we have 24 hour days if the earth actually rotates every 23 hours and 56 minutes?" One smart person responded, "23 hours and 56 minutes is one 'sidereal' day with respect to the stars, but by then the Earth is in a slightly different position in its orbit around the Sun, so it takes an extra 4 minutes to make one 'solar' day (the number of sidereal days in a year is exactly one greater than the number of solar days)."[5] I didn't really understand that much at all. But at the very least we can say that each of us has 23 hours and 56 minutes every day to experience. And to use.

The more critical question is not how much time we have, but who's in charge of our time? What I mean is, if I am a follower of Jesus, time belongs to Him. *My* time belongs to Him. I am to be "on mission." That means each day ought to begin with my saying, "Lord, how will you deploy me today? Make me aware of the seconds and minutes that I should invest in doing Kingdom business on this day called 'today.'"

If that were my attitude every day (and it sadly isn't), I would look at each encounter with other human beings as opportunities to sow some seed, to share a bit about the Lord, to intentionally listen to their stories. And that takes time.

Can we talk? If we Christians were really honest, we would like nothing better than to hang around only with other Christians, listen only to Christian music, read only Christian books, and eat only Christian cookies. We don't want to be around pagans, ex-

---

5   https://www.quora.com/Why-do-we-have-24-hour-days-if-the-earth-
     actually-rotates-every-23-hours-and-56-minutes

cept to invite them once in a while to our churches for Christian casseroles.

How did Jesus spend His time? Of course He spent a significant amount of His days and nights with His disciples, but, socially, He invested Himself in "those who [were] sick, who [needed] a physician." This included the secular sick as well as the religiously sick.

Years ago I got to serve on a committee which was searching for a new dean for our seminary. I was tasked to interview an in-house applicant and I asked him only two questions: (1) "What do you do for fun?", and (2) "Please tell me about your unsaved friends." He responded honestly to both questions and said: "I don't do anything for fun" and "I don't have any unsaved friends."

We will look at the serious issue of having fun with lost friends in an appendix, but I found his two answers alarming. Although many would assume that a seminary dean should look like he just came out of a cave-like monastery, wearing a long robe tied around his waist with a rope belt and munching on locusts, that is hardly the picture we get of the Lord Jesus. He enjoyed being around unbelievers. And there is evidence that He laughed with them and appreciated their company. As Elton Trueblood makes clear in his book The *Humour of Christ*, Jesus was not just a man of sorrows. Although we have no verse that says, "And Jesus laughed," part of His humanity was that He could be quite comfortable around the non-religious. Trueblood is right when he says that we are wrong when we make the sad story the whole story.

I've been working hard over the last few years to spend time with those who need the Lord. I got saved as a teenager and promptly lost most of my unsaved friends because I thought I should hang around only with other Christians, listen only to Christian music, read only Christian books, and eat only Christian cookies. Some studies have shown that new converts lose all their non-Christian friends within the first year of their conversion. And the church is often quite willing to help with that process.

I have so much to learn about being a "friend" of sinners. I think many of us Jesus-followers would flunk Friendship 101 if we had to take such a course. But I'm working at it. I purposely join tennis teams where I'm probably the only believer. I'm thrilled when one of my tennis buddies calls me in great frustration to talk about how his new banister kit for his stairs he ordered from China isn't complete, or another friend going into detail about his wife's cataract surgery, or the lady who waits on me at Starbucks complaining that the new shingles on her house are going to cost her a fortune. I'm into *investing*. I'm learning to listen. And sometimes, just sometimes, they ask my opinion. They want to hear my perspective. And I can tell them a little about Jesus.

Being All There

By the way, I'm also slowly learning that unless I have somewhere else that I need to be, I'm purposely letting the other person end the conversation. Looking at my phone or at my watch is a sure-fire way to say to the other person in no uncertain terms, "You're not really that important to me right now. Can we conclude our time together?"

Many Christians are quite familiar with the missionary/martyr Jim Elliot's statement when he said, "He is no fool who gives what he cannot keep to gain what he cannot lose." That's a wonderful quote. [I once taught a preaching course in Bible college and I told the students that if they are using such a quote in their sermon and they mess it up, just keep going! Sure enough, one student said, "He is no fool who loses what he never had to gain what he cannot keep." I was roaring with laughter inside, but I was proud of him because he kept going!].

There's another famous Jim Elliot quote that is worth pondering. He said, "Wherever you are, be all there. Live to the hilt every moment you believe to be the will of God." When we seek to multitask or are not giving the person in front of us our best attention, we are simply "not all there." I'm learning, slowly, to focus on the other person and to develop serious friendships.

What a joy to have a lost person calling me! And that involves spending a lot of time listening to their problems and issues. Time. One writer said, "Time is free, but it's priceless. You can't own it, but you can use it. You can't keep it, but you can spend it. Once you've lost it you can never get it back." (Harvey MacKay).

Spirituality and Steve Jobs

I started to read Steve Jobs' biography, but gave up when I couldn't seem to find any spiritual interest in the late Apple co-founder's life. When he died he was worth about $10 billion. But he did say something interesting about time:

> "Your time is limited, so don't waste it living someone else's life. Don't be trapped by dogma — which is living with the results of other people's thinking. Don't let the noise of other's opinions drown out your own inner voice. And most important, have the courage to follow your heart and intuition. They somehow already know what you truly want to become. Everything else is secondary."

There's a bit of wisdom in Jobs' statement. And a large dose of foolishness. Christians are not "trapped by dogma." We've been privileged to come to know the Savior and to learn His truths. And one's inner voice? That voice gets me into a bunch of trouble at times.

I love the statement by the late humorist Erma Bombeck who said, "I went out and bought the book *How to Be Your Own Best Friend*, gained twenty pounds, and haven't trusted myself since." Jobs says we are to follow our hearts and intuition. Scripture says, "The heart is deceitful above all things and beyond cure. Who can understand it?" (Jeremiah 17:9). Putting God and His Word is primary. Everything else is secondary!

How I spend my time is how I spend my life. Jim Rohn once said, "Time is more valuable than money. You can get more money, but you cannot get more time." Jesus spent time with sinners. How are you going to invest your time today?

A Challenge:

We each have the same amount of time everyday. How we spend our time is how we spend our lives. You're heard the illustration that says that no businessman on his deathbed wishes, "Wow, I wish I'd spent more time at work!" How about you and me? On our deathbeds, will we wish, "I regret I spent so little time with those who need the Lord Jesus"?

As I have mentioned, I love the sport of tennis and being on a team forces me to invest hours with other people. It puts me in situations in which I can represent the Lord. Are there temptations to lose my temper, to blame others for losses, to become impatient with other players? Of course. But life is filled with risk. And when I blow it as a believer, I want to be quick to apologize and move on.

What sport or activity do you enjoy? Do it with unbelievers! Determine before the Lord that you are going to do something you love and you are going to do it with those who need to see your life as a believer.

Questions for Chapter Three:

1. What was wrong with Simon the Pharisee's logic in Luke 7?

2. What practical step can you take to overcome the excuse, "I just don't have time to spend with lost people"?

3. If you could choose to join a sports team or a hobby club, what would it be? What's keeping you from joining?

CHAPTER FOUR:

"BEFORE YOU JUDGE ME, TAKE A LOOK AT YO-SELF ..." ♫

(Eric Clapton)

"I like constructive criticism from smart people." (Prince)

"To avoid criticism, do nothing, say nothing, and be nothing." (Elbert Hubbard)

"In this life you sometimes have to choose between pleasing God and pleasing man. In the long run it's better to please God — He's more apt to remember." (Harry Kemelman)

Can we talk? We fear men much more than we fear God! We are afraid that if we hang out with pagans, our Christian "friends" will assume things about us and our names will be at the top of the prayer lists of small groups as they pray for the "needs" and "struggles" of the body.

Jesus never let criticism deter Him from doing what He came to do: to seek and to save that which was lost. And His greatest criticism came not from unbelievers, but from "believers" who couldn't handle His irritating persistence of spending time with sinners.

"Good to Go!"

A retired pastor of a growing church tells about how he had invested time in a particular friend who was far from God. Every Christmas the pastor's family would have this man and his wife over for Christmas dinner — and they would simply live out their Christian lives before them.

One Christmas, as the man was getting their coats to head home after a delicious dinner, he said to the pastor, "Just want you to know: I'm good to go!" The pastor said, "What? Good to go?

What do you mean?" "I've trusted Christ as my Savior. So I'm good to go. Ready to serve. Thanks for the dinner."

As he tells the story, the pastor weeps as he thinks back to his investment of time and energy in that relationship. "I could have missed all that," he says. "But, by God's grace, I got to be a part of that man's coming to Christ! There is no greater Christmas present than that!"

In this book we are talking about investing our lives in the lives of those who are, in this pastor's words, "far from God." It would be quite an enlightening experiment to keep a record of how many hours per week you and I spend with lost people. How many hours do we spend with the saved? How many hours do we spend by ourselves?

Just as our checkbooks show what is important to us in life, so our schedules and our calendars and our watches display the use of our time. But criticism will come. Let me tell you about one of the most painful experiences of my life.

A Hometown Surprise

Years ago I used to preach at my home church in another state every few months. I thought my sermons were being well received. But I remember being in my driveway and getting a call on my cell. It turned out to be the head elder from my home church and he said there had been some complaints about my preaching.

I was totally taken by surprise. Then I realized I was on speaker phone before my home church's elders' meeting! (holy ambush!) I tried to compose myself and then asked, "What are the concerns about my ministry?" The head elder listed three: (1) Some think you should not refer positively to counseling; (2) Some believe you were wrong to have leaders of various cults come to your "Eternal Destinies" seminary class to lecture, and (3) Some thought you speak too often of Christians' needing to have unsaved friends.

I was floored and, trying not to sound defensive, felt I needed to respond briefly to each of those "charges." "Well," I said, "to the concern that I refer positively to counseling, I believe some

Christians need professional help but it should come from those who are sympathetic to our Christian convictions. Regarding the second 'concern,' I had the permission of my seminary dean to invite representatives from the Jehovah's Witnesses and the Mormons and Christian Science and others to my upper-level theology class. My students," I said, "were not converted to those cults, you need to know!"

Other than the clearing of a few throats, I didn't get any response from the elders who had me on the phone. I continued, "Concerning my frequent reference to Christians' needing to have unsaved friends, I won't back down from that an inch! We are too cloistered, too cocooned in our Christian cliques, too unlike the Lord Jesus who came _for_ sinners!"

I then told the head elder that I would travel to my home church (over a three-hour drive) to meet face-to-face with those who had those concerns. "Would you please arrange that meeting?", I asked him.

A week later he told me that those people would not agree to meet with me and the elders. I said, "You're one of the primary spiritual leaders of the church and they're turning you down? God wants us to seek reconciliation with each other." He said, "They refuse to meet. They just wanted to express their concerns."

I was quite disappointed, but accepted the church's invitation to speak a couple of times over the next few months. I only found out later that when I would come to preach, one of the critics would stay for the early service of communion, but then leave before the second service so he didn't have to be under my preaching. How sad. _And he was the man the Lord had used to lead me to faith when I was a teenager._

That whole episode broke my heart. I forgave those who were criticizing me. A couple of years later that man who led me to Christ began staying for my preaching. I guess he worked it out with the Lord.

Criticism hurts. It stings. And especially so when God's method of reconciliation isn't followed. But expect criticism. From your brethren. And others.

Criticism Avoidance

The late musician Prince put it this way: "I like constructive criticism from smart people." Apparently no one criticized the multi-millionaire rock icon for his opioid drug use, for he died of an apparent overdose on April 21, 2016.

Prince sold more than 100 million records, won seven Grammys and was inducted into the Rock and Roll Hall of Fame in 2004.

Although Prince (born Prince Rogers Nelson) said he valued constructive criticism, he, like all of us, likely preferred positive feedback from the people around him. "The trouble with most of us," Norman Vincent Peale once said, "is that we would rather be ruined by praise than saved by criticism."

A Criticized Christ

In what ways was Jesus criticized? He was certainly criticized for His claims of deity (could forgive sins, etc.). And He was criticized for healing on the Sabbath (two areas that we will not be criticized for). But He was specifically chastised for spending time with and eating with sinners. Let's look at several examples of His being criticized for His culinary custom of dining with (what the Pharisees saw as) the damned.

When I eat and get criticized, it is usually about my eating too much or not trying new dishes or talking with my mouth full or using the wrong fork. I don't think I've ever been criticized for eating with certain other people.

Jesus' choice of His dinner companions was challenged in Luke 5 by the Pharisees and the teachers of the law who didn't have the courtesy to speak to Jesus directly. They complained to the disciples, "Why do you eat and drink with tax collectors and sinners?" (v. 30). The "you" there is plural, so they were criticizing both Jesus and His disciples.

Whether He was within earshot or He read their minds, Jesus was aware of their accusatory question and responded, "It is not the healthy who need a doctor, but the sick. I have not come to call the righteous, but sinners to repentance." (vv. 31-32). Jesus was challenged for allowing this "great banquet" to be arranged for Him at Levi's house and specifically for eating with "a large crowd of tax collectors and others" (v. 29).

Sometimes Jesus' dinner guests included formerly demon-possessed women! We read in Luke 8 that He was accompanied by the Twelve as He traveled from town to town, as well as by "some women who had been cured of evil spirits and diseases" (v. 2). He even allowed them to support Him and the disciples out of their own means.

Who's the Real Prodigal?

One of the most blatant examples of Jesus being criticized is given to us in the famous story which Jesus told. The story of the prodigal son (Luke 15) focuses upon the issue of <u>lostness</u> and is the third illustration (after the lost sheep and the lost coin) of something valued which needed to be found.[6]

But these three stories of lostness are told by the Lord Jesus specifically because He was being criticized by the religious leaders of His day. Luke 15 begins with this introduction: "Now the tax collectors and sinners were all gathering around to hear Jesus. But the Pharisees and the teachers of the law muttered, 'This man welcomes sinners and eats with them'" (verses 1-2).

Occasionally when my wife and I are pooped on a Friday night, she'll send me out for pizza. I'll come home and announce, "The hunter and the gatherer has returned! Let's feast!" Men like

---

6   I have discussed Luke 15 extensively in my book *DocWALK: Putting into Practice What You Say You Believe* (Christian Focus, 2005).

to hunt and gather, so long as pizza is involved and we don't have to wear heavy winter camouflage or carry weapons.

Jesus was a hunter and a gatherer! He *gathered* the tax collectors and sinners together, for He sought them out. They loved to hear Him. Others, however, chose not to gather but to mutter.

Muttering Disapproval

I'm not very good at muttering, but I'm working on it. Muttering is defined as "to utter words indistinctly or in a low tone, often as if talking to oneself; to murmur."

Very rarely my wife might ask me to do something which I don't want to do at the moment (like leave my perfectly comfortable recliner to fetch something completely unnecessary for her, like her glasses) and I might, just might, engage in a bit of muttering. She will then say, "Do I hear you *muttering*?" I'll say, "No! Well, yes. But I didn't mean to do that out loud." "Well, it *was* out loud and I heard you," she will say. And we will laugh. (Mostly, I will laugh. Nervously. Then I'll fetch her glasses. This woman has the power to starve me to death if she so chooses.)

Usually the only low, rumbling sound I make is a completely involuntary noise from my insides proclaiming that I am hungry. But before I ask my wife for food I ask her if I can go fetch something for her.

The religious leaders mutter when they see the crowds of tax collectors and sinners gathered around Jesus to listen to Him. And their muttering is quite specific: "This man welcomes sinners and eats with them" (v. 2).[7]

Jesus then gives three stories of lost items, appealing to the panic of anyone who has lost anything of value! The lost sheep (vv. 3-7) could have been written off as expendable, but the shepherd leaves his 99 sheep to search for this one. It meant something to

---

7   I've had Christian groups from New York to Myanmar practice muttering that statement: "This man welcomes sinners and eats with them." They scrunch up their faces and snarl those words. It is quite delightful to see them throw themselves into the role!

him. And when he finds it, he throws a party and people, presumably other shepherds, join him in celebrating. (I would have barbecued that renegade sheep, but that's just me).

The lost coin (vv. 8-10) might have had intrinsic value, but commentators tell us it was probably part of an elaborate head dress — and it meant a great deal to the woman. She goes to some effort to sweep her house and when she finds it, she invites her neighbors to rejoice with her.

In both the lost sheep and the lost coin stories *rejoicing* is prominent. God wants lost things found! I rejoice when I have found an important lost item. How about you?

My mother-in-law never loses anything. She knows where everything she owns is. Her walk-in closet would impress Martha Stewart. Mom can close her eyes and tell you what is on every shelf. I once said to my mother-in-law, "Mom, you know, you are so organized you never experience the joy of finding something. *'Cause you know where everything is!* That's just a sad way to live!" She laughs at me and changes the subject.

When the lost sheep is found, the shepherd calls his friends and neighbors and they have a party. When the woman finds her lost coin (after sweeping the house from top to bottom), she calls her friends and neighbors to celebrate with her.

But at the conclusion of each of these stories, Jesus adds a moral about lost *people*. At the end of the story of the lost sheep Jesus says, "I tell you that in the same way there will be more rejoicing in heaven over one sinner who repents than over ninety-nine righteous persons who do not need to repent" (v. 7). At the end of the story of the lost coin, He says, "In the same way, I tell you, there is rejoicing in the presence of the angels of God over one sinner who repents" (v. 10).

Surprisingly, the story of the prodigal son could very well be renamed "The Story of the Older Brother." While the younger son turned his back on his family and went off and majored in serious debauchery, the older brother was faithful to his father and worked hard on the farm.

The return of the broke and broken younger brother was met by a forgiving father who threw a massive party. The older brother did not join in the festivities, but was out in the field working (v. 25). He not only boycotts the party but actually *rebukes* his father for celebrating his renegade brother's return. He pleads his own faithfulness — "Look! All these years I've been slaving for you and never disobeyed your orders. Yet you never gave me even a young goat so I could celebrate with my friends." (v. 29).

But the father challenges the older son's outrage. "My son," he says, "you are always with me, and everything I have is yours. But we had to celebrate and be glad, because this brother of yours was dead and is alive again; he was lost and is found." (vv. 31-32).

And that's how this most famous story ends. Is there any doubt that Jesus was specifically talking about the Pharisees and the teachers of the law who had muttered, "This man welcomes sinners and eats with them"? Not only did they refuse to join Jesus' search party for lost people, but they criticized Him for His reaching out to them. Their "faithfulness" to God kept them out working on the farm instead of rejoicing in the father's mercy and extravagant love.

When God says "Party!", we'd better party. Unless we don't care about lost people.

Count on It!

Count on the fact that you will be criticized by other Christians if you become a serious friend of sinners. Spending time with lost people might make you miss a church meeting or two — and that's a sure sign of backsliding in many churches.

The movie director Mel Brooks was asked what he thought about critics. He said, "When you are camping in the woods at night, they are very loud and they make it quite difficult to get to sleep." "No," said the interviewer, "I didn't say *crickets*. I said *critics*!" "They're even worse," Brooks said. "They can't even rub their back legs together and make music!"

But the healthier churches, instead of criticizing, will encourage their people to get out there and develop relationships with those who need the Lord. The growing churches are those which re-alize that we are called to be part of Jesus' search and rescue mission. Spiritually-minded church leaders are those who set the example by spending significant time with those who need Christ — and they are not reluctant to ask for prayer for those relationships.

My dream is that churches and their leaders would say to their members something like the following:

> "We're glad you're part of this church. But we want you to be a friend of sinners like Jesus was. What do you enjoy doing? What activity or sport would you pursue if you took the time and if we encouraged you to make it a priority in your life? Then go do it — to the glory of God!"

Questions for Chapter Four:

1. Why are we so afraid of criticism — especially from other believers?

2. In the story of the prodigal son, who's the real prodigal? Why?

3. Do you agree with my dream that I share at the end of this chapter? What would you change (if anything)?

CHAPTER FIVE:

"HONESTY — IT'S SUCH A LONELY WORD!" 🎵

(Billy Joel)

"We have, in a real sense, lost sense of the lostness of the lost!" (Francis Schaeffer)

"When I was 12," writes Sylvester Madison, "my best friend and I broke a window playing baseball. We looked around to see if anyone had seen us. No one was in sight except my younger brother. We went over and offered him a piece of candy not to tell. He refused it. `I'll give you my baseball,' I said. `No.' `Then what about *my* baseball and my new glove?' my friend added. `No!' `Well, what *do* you want?' `I wanna tell.'"

"Jesus looked at him and loved him. `One thing you lack,' he said. `Go, sell everything you have and give to the poor, and you will have treasure in heaven. Then come, follow me.'" (Mark 10:21)

Can we talk? Unsaved people often drive me crazy! They throw around my Savior's name like some cheap swearword from the gutter. Some of them drink like fish. They fool around outside their marriages. And they smell.

I was kidding about that last one. Actually, one of the things that drives me most crazy about lost friends is their . . . goodness. Some of my friends have literally given me the shirt off their backs when our house burned down. One of my tennis buddies didn't hesitate coming over to my house when I had a problem with my lawn mower. Another friend plays tennis with me even though he creams me every time. These are good people. And they drive me crazy!

Why? Because the Bible says they are sinners in need of a Savior. And part of my job is helping them to see that. When they define sin as murder and rape, it's difficult to convince them of their sinnership when they haven't done those things. These are people who will donate to good causes, attend the funerals of friends who pass away, and collect my mail when we're on vacation. And I'm supposed to tell them they need to get *saved?*

Reaching Good People

How in the world do we reach <u>good</u> people? And, honestly, do we want to put in that much hard work?

Jesus met a young man who was really into goodness. Let's notice how the Lord handled the situation. We read in Mark 10:17-27,

> 17 As Jesus started on his way, a man ran up to him and fell on his knees before him. "Good teacher," he asked, "what must I do to inherit eternal life?" 18 "Why do you call me good?" Jesus answered. "No one is good—except God alone. 19 You know the commandments: 'You shall not murder, you shall not commit adultery, you shall not steal, you shall not give false testimony, you shall not defraud, honor your father and mother.'" 20 "Teacher," he declared, "all these I have kept since I was a boy." 21 Jesus looked at him and loved him. "One thing you lack," he said. "Go, sell everything you have and give to the poor, and you will have treasure in heaven. Then come, follow me." 22 At this the man's face fell. He went away sad, because he had great wealth. 23 Jesus looked around and said to his disciples, "How hard it is for the rich to enter the king-dom of God!" 24 The disciples were amazed at his words. But Jesus said again, "Children, how hard it is to enter the kingdom of God! 25 It is easier for a camel to go through the eye of a needle than for someone who is rich to enter the kingdom of God." 26 The disciples were even more amazed, and said to each other, "Who then can be saved?" 27 Jesus looked at them and said, "With man this is impossible, but not with God; all things are possible with God."

A Critical Question

This story of the rich young ruler is told us in all three synoptic gospels. I'm sure you use the word "synoptic" every day, but some readers might need it defined. "Synoptic" literally means to see the same. Matthew, Mark, and Luke basically cover the same material in the life of Jesus (about 94% of the gospel of John is unique to his account).

We will point out a few differences (not contradictions) in the three gospels' accounts, but let us follow Mark's presentation of this encounter.

I've never had someone run up to me, fall on their knees, and ask me a question. But that's what this man does in Mark 10. Matthew just says "a man came up to Jesus" (Matthew 19:16) and Luke describes the encounter as "a certain ruler asked him" (Luke 18:18). Mark's account is a bit more dramatic, for it says "a man ran up to him and fell on his knees before him."

"My Goodness!"

This man, this certain ruler, bursts on the scene, interrupting Jesus' travel plans, to ask Him one question. If you could ask Jesus one question, what would it be? His question (as Mark and Luke describe it) is: "Good teacher, what must I do to inherit eternal life?" (v. 17). Matthew, however, records the question as "Teacher, what good thing must I do to get eternal life?" (Matthew 19:16).

There is no contradiction here. Mark (and Luke) record one question; Matthew a second question. Perhaps in his hurriedness to stop Jesus and ask what was most important to him this ruler blurts out both questions in a rapid-fire way: "Good teacher, what must I do to inherit eternal life?" and "Teacher, what good thing must I do to get eternal life?" He clearly wanted eternal life and thought that goodness had a lot to do with getting it!

A Surprising Response

Jesus' response in Mark's and Luke's accounts is: "Why do you call me good? No one is good — except God alone." Matthew records Jesus' response as "Why do you ask me about what is good?" If only God is good, we do not believe that it is too strong to say that the point Jesus is making is this: To call Jesus "good" is to call Jesus "God"! For only God is truly good.

But this man was into goodness. He wanted to either inherit or earn eternal life. And he knew it had something to do with being good or doing good. Little did he realize that no one could be that good. And Jesus will help him with this truth.

A Selective List

After His unusual response ("Why do you call me good?" and "Why do you ask me about what is good?"), Jesus brings up the Jews' well-known criterion for goodness — God's commandments.

In both Mark's and Luke's accounts, Jesus says "You know the commandments." In Matthew's account, Jesus says, "If you want to enter life, keep the commandments." (Matthew 19:17). To keep them the ruler had to know them.

Jesus then lists the commandments, but *not all of them*. And His list is quite interesting! In Mark's account, Jesus lists **six** commandments: don't murder, don't commit adultery, don't steal, don't give false testimony, don't defraud, and honor your father and mother. In Luke's account, Jesus lists **five** commandments: don't commit adultery, don't murder, don't steal, don't give false testimony, and honor your father and mother. In Matthew's account, Jesus lists **six** commandments: don't murder, don't commit adultery, don't steal, don't give false testimony, honor father and mother, and love your neighbor as yourself!

There are a lot of interesting differences in the three accounts, but let's not miss the main point. Why does Jesus list *these* commandments, but not the others?

Which ones *does* He list? If we look at the list of the Ten Commandments in Exodus 20 and Deuteronomy 5, we see that Jesus lists commandments #'s 5-9. He does not list commandments #'s 1-4 or #10. What's the significance?

Mark 10	Matthew 19	Luke 18
don't murder	don't murder	no adultery
no adultery	no adultery	don't murder
don't steal	don't steal	don't steal
no false witness	no false witness	no false witness
don't defraud	honor f & m	honor f & m
honor f & m	love neighbor as self	

Remember that in Matthew's account, the man responds to Jesus' statement "If you want to enter life, keep the commandments" by asking, "which ones?" (Matthew 19:18).

Jesus lists the commandments that relate to <u>man</u>: not murdering (#6), not committing adultery (#7), not stealing (#8), not giving a false witness (#9), and honoring one's father and mother (#5). He does not list: no other gods before me (#1), no graven images (#2), don't misuse God's name (#3), remember the Sabbath (#4), and don't covet (#10).

An Amazing Declaration

After Jesus gives His selective list, the ruler says, "Teacher, all these I have kept since I was a boy." (Mark 10:20; Luke 18:21). Matthew records the ruler's response as: "All these I have kept.

What do I still lack?" (Matthew 19:20). Ahhh, a great question: "What do I still *lack*?"

Perhaps the ruler was not aware of Jesus' so-called "Sermon on the Mount" in which He broadened the definition of murder to include anger in one's heart (Matthew 5:21-22) and of adultery to include lustful thoughts (Matthew 5:27-28). As a fallen human being, he was certainly guilty of both of these sins!

But in terms of outward behavior, we have no reason to doubt his testimony about himself that he had not committed murder or adultery or born false witness or engaged in thievery, but had consistently honored his parents. He had been a good boy and was now an exemplary human being.

In many ways, this man was goodness personified. But he had to ask Jesus his question about getting or inheriting eternal life. If righteousness were graded on a curve, this man had it made. Jesus should have said to him, "You're *good* to go!" But he wasn't.

Before Jesus lowers the boom and this man learns of his lack, the gospel of Mark uniquely points something out. Something that Matthew and Luke don't include. But something very important to the story. Mark includes the statement: "Jesus looked at him and loved him" (Mark 10:21). One might reasonably say, "Of course, Jesus loved him. Jesus loves everyone." But that would miss the point. Mark includes this detail just before Jesus says, "One thing you lack."

But, wait a minute! That's why the man stopped Jesus in His tracks, running up to Him with his question, right? He wanted to know what he could do to inherit eternal life. Now Jesus is going to tell him. But Jesus is going to tell him out of love.

An Almost Impossible Requirement

On the surface Evangelicals are a bit uncomfortable with what Jesus next says to this man. One sect of Christianity says that Jesus is inviting this man into becoming a kind of co-redeemer by keeping God's law.

Instead of challenging him to believe and forsake his trust in his own goodness, Jesus gives him an assignment — something to *do*. Talk about works-salvation!

But the Lord's wisdom is far greater than our foolishness, and He knows what He's doing. He gives this command out of love, knowing how the man will respond.

Jesus' command is simple: "Go, sell everything you have and give to the poor, and you will have treasure in heaven. Then come, follow me." Matthew's account is a bit different: "*If you want to be perfect*, go, sell your possessions and give to the poor, and you will have treasure in heaven. Then come, follow me." Luke adds the words, "You still lack one thing."

What would have been involved in this man's doing what Jesus told him to do? Notice the steps:

"Go!" He would have to leave Jesus physically to do what Jesus told him to do.

"Sell everything you have . . ." This man would have had to organize a massive garage sale (we learn in Mark 10:22 that he had "great wealth." Luke's account tells us that he was "very wealthy").

"And give to the poor . . ." This man would not be allowed to keep any of the proceeds from his gigantic garage sale. He would have to turn over the cold, hard cash to "the poor," those who would be unable to pay him back. This might have involved his seeking out the poor. Perhaps he knew very few in this category.

"And you will have treasure in heaven . . ." Earthly treasure can steal our hearts. Jesus is offering this man an opportunity to trade his earthly wealth for a heavenly reward. He would have to give up his stuff if he were going to trust the Savior.

"Then come, follow me." The last step to be taken was to become a poor, dependent disciple, following a rejected rabbi and joining a motley crew of strangers.

Mark's account tells us that "at this the man's face fell" (v. 22). And, without a word of reply to Jesus, "he went away sad, because he had great wealth" (v. 22).

An Unfortunate Decision

Our emotions show the condition of our hearts, don't they? We read that this young ruler, when he heard the steps Jesus set out for him, "became very sad, because he was very wealthy." (Luke 18:23). Sadness does not have to be a permanent state, but it was the impetus for this man to walk away from Jesus. And without a word of reply to the Lord, "he went away sad, because he had great wealth" (Matthew 19:22).

Luke's account tells us that "Jesus looked at him and said, 'How hard it is for the rich to enter the kingdom of God!'" (v. 24). Mark tells us that "Jesus looked around and said [those words] to his disciples."

An Amazing Analogy

The Lord then gives an amazing analogy. He says, "It is easier for a camel to go through the eye of a needle than for someone who is rich to enter the kingdom of God." Contrary to some popular preaching, the "eye of the needle" was not a gate in Jerusalem which opened after the main gate was closed. The rumor was that a camel could only pass through this smaller gate if it had its baggage removed and got on its knees to crawl through the gate. This story, popular since the 15th century, lacks any accepted evidence of its existence. And such a story actually contradicts the point that Jesus is making.

The word for "camel" in this passage means camel. The word for "needle" means sewing needle. Which hump of the camel would be pushed first through the eye of a sewing needle? Such a feat would be impossible!

What is impossible for man — and for a camel — is possible for God! It is *God* who saves, not man saving himself through his wealth or his good works.

In the minds of the disciples, wealth meant God's blessing. Wealthy, good people need to be reminded of what they "lack."

And that message, the message of the grace of God in the gospel, will sometimes only result in others walking away.

By the way, please notice that Jesus doesn't chase the young ruler to renegotiate the terms of salvation. He lets him walk away. Good, religious people need to see that their goodness falls short of the glory of God and they need to repent of their sins and trust the only One who is truly good — Jesus.

Hard Honesty . . . and Comfort!

How do we become honest with our good, lost friends? How do we help those good people we know, who may even attend church or read their Bibles, to understand that their goodness won't save them?

Oh, sure, we can quote Ephesians 2:8-9 to them: "8For it is by grace you have been saved, through faith—and this is not from yourselves, it is the gift of God— 9 not by works, so that no one can boast." We can point out that no one will be saved by his or her sincere efforts at keeping God's laws. We can certainly explain that God's commandments were never given to earn us forgiveness, but rather to show us our sin.

Ray Comfort, to me, is a great example of one who uses the law of God lawfully. He is not reluctant to engage in conversations with people on the street to ask them if they think they are good people. Many say, "Yes, I'm a good person."

He will then ask them if they have ever lied. Most will say, "Of course, I've lied." "What do you call someone who lies?", he will ask. "A liar," the person will say.

"Have you ever taken something that didn't belong to you?" "Yes, I have." "What do you call someone who steals?" "A thief!"

He will then ask them if they have ever lusted after another person in their heart. Some will say, "Well, I guess so." He will tell them that the Bible says that those who lust after another in their heart are guilty of adultery. "So what do you call someone who commits adultery?", he will ask. "An adulterer?"

He will then ask them if they have ever used God's name in vain. "Sure. Hasn't everybody?", they might say. Comfort will then say, "Such a person is called a blasphemer."

Then he will ask, "Where do you think lying, thieving, lusting blasphemers go when they die?" Some will honestly answer, "Hell?" Then he shares the Good News of the gospel with them.

Getting Personal

I appreciate Comfort's approach — and he gets plenty of people furious by his logical and straightforward questions.[8] I would suggest that he — and we — speak about how we deserved God's eternal judgment, that we have been guilty of lying, stealing, lusting, and blaspheming.

Too often those who are outside of God's family feel like Christians are looking to poke their finger into their chest and call them "SINNERS!" If we don't add the autobiographical part about ourselves, it may sound like we think we are holier than the lost person.

We need to reach good people with the gospel. We must help them see that there are no small sins before a holy God.

---

8   You can watch several of his on-the-street encounters on YouTube. Here's one: https://www.youtube.com/watch?v=GSvGGkPQgh0

Questions for Chapter Five:

1. Why is it so hard to be honest about the gospel with the "good" people we know?

2. The rich young ruler in Mark 10 — what was his real problem, do you think?

3. Do you agree with Ray Comfort's approach in witnessing? What is he seeking to accomplish?

4. What witnessing strategies have you found to be effective? Ineffective? Should we have "strategies" at all? Why or why not?

CHAPTER SIX:

"HOW CAN IT BE WRONG . . . WHEN IT FEELS SO RIGHT?" 🎵

(Debbie Boone)

"When you have to start compromising yourself or your morals for the people around you, it's probably time to change the people around you." (Anonymous)

"Don't compromise yourself. You are all you've got." (Janis Joplin)

"Compromise is a sign you'll pass on the road to mediocrity." (Tim Fargo)

Mahatma Gandhi said: "All compromise is based on give and take, but there can be no give and take on fundamentals. Any compromise on mere fundamentals is a surrender. For it is all give and no take."

We are seeking to make the case in this book that we are unlike Jesus in that we aren't friends of sinners like He was. We isolate ourselves from the lost, we try to avoid the world, and we hang around only with other Christians.

If we hang out with others at all. You need to know that I test out as an introvert. I've taken the Myers/Briggs, the Briggs and Stratton, and other personality tests and the verdict comes back, "My goodness! You're an INTROVERT!" Now, I'm what they call an expressive introvert. I can mingle with the best of them, but I'm worn out afterwards. My daughter is also an introvert and she threatens to buy us matching t-shirts that say, "INTROVERTS UNITE! IN YOUR OWN HOMES! BY YOURSELVES!"

I served as an interim preaching pastor in a small church for over a year and loved it. But one of the hard things that I did was greet people before the service every Sunday. I would have been much more comfortable staying in a back room, lighting a candle, praying and going over my message, but that wasn't the course I chose. I chose to shake hands with strangers, to tease a group of older ladies, to welcome people to the service, and to be, well, uncomfortable.

And now the Lord is having me write a book on developing friendships with lost people! What a sense of humor the Lord has. But I'm baby stepping.

A Quick Review

Some of our problem is a misunderstanding of the world. We are not to be friends of the world in the sense of the pagan system opposing God and the things of God. But to be a friend of sinners is not the same as being a friend of the world. Some believers are deathly afraid of worldliness and think that isolation is the answer. The Corinthian believers did — and they compromised both evangelism and discipleship by their misunderstanding.

Time is a primary reason why many of us don't develop relationships with lost people. Demands on our time are everywhere. And sometimes the greatest obstacle to investing in connections with those who need Christ . . . is the local church! A Christian leader years ago wrote a short book entitled *Stop the Meetings! I Want to Get Off!* He was soundly criticized for that book (by the extremely faithful church goers), but he had an excellent point.

None of us likes criticism and we've seen how rough Christians can be with one another. So to avoid criticism from the family we avoid the very ones not yet in the family Jesus left us here to reach!

The truth is that many of our unsaved friends are good people. And the task of honestly convincing them of their sinnership and need of Christ is challenging! Super-religious people are lost too and need to be shown that they do not merit heaven with their goodness and that their badness, like ours, deserves God's eternal wrath. And that's tough to do. C.S. Lewis makes the argument that we should do everything in our power to produce a world where as many people as possible grow up nice. He then says, "A world of nice people, content in their own niceness, looking no further, turned away from God, would be just as desperately in need of salvation as a miserable world—and might even be more difficult to save."[9]

The Challenge of Compromise

It may be that for some a fear of compromise is the barrier to developing friendships with the lost. To be sure, a believer who struggled (or continues to struggle) with alcoholism shouldn't look at the local bar as his or her mission field. Backsliding is not an evangelistic requirement or technique!

How do we avoid compromise? We get some insight on this issue as we think about an amazing text in I Corinthians 10. There we read —

> 27 If an unbeliever invites you to a meal and you want to go, eat whatever is put before you without raising questions of conscience. 28 But if someone says to you, "This has been offered in sacrifice," then do not eat it, both for the sake of the one who told you and for the sake of conscience. 29 I am referring to the other person's conscience, not yours. For why is my freedom being judged by another's conscience? 30 If I take part in the meal with thankfulness, why am I denounced because of something I thank God for? 31 So whether you eat or drink or whatever you do, do it all for the glory of God. 32 Do not cause anyone to stumble, whether Jews, Greeks or the church of God— 33 even as I try to please everyone in every way. For I am not seeking my own good but the good of many, so that they may be saved.

An Incredible Invitation

This is a fascinating passage for a variety of reasons. Notice that the believer is invited by an unbeliever to a meal (v. 27). Oh, that we believers would receive more invitations to meals from unbelievers! And Paul does not waffle on the term "unbeliever."

---

9   C.S. Lewis, *Mere Christianity* (1952; Harper Collins: 2001) 215-216.

This is clearly an invitation from someone outside the family of God to someone inside the family of God to have a meal together.

Are you being invited over to the homes of unsaved people for dinner? Or to watch the Super Bowl? Or to play boardgames? Why not? It might be that they have been taken captive by the same time-monster as many Christians. We work two or three jobs, have dinner (sometimes) with our families, then collapse into our LazyBoy recliners to let the blue light of the big screen TV wash over us until we drag ourselves to bed. The next day repeats itself, much like a kind of "Groundhog's Day" script.

We must get a grip on the use of our time. But I imagine most Christians would not say that they are routinely turning down invitations to their lost friends' homes because they don't have the time. They would say, if they were brutally honest, that they are simply not being invited.

Invitations are often reciprocal. If you or I invite our unsaved friends to our homes for a meal, they will often respond in kind. I live down South. Traditionally homes down here used to be built with large wraparound front porches so neighbors could get together, drink some sweet tea, and tell each other stories about the crazy things their children were doing. Today it seems that the homes of many Christians are not so inviting. They look more like castles with a drawbridge (raised, not lowered) over a moat (fully stocked with hungry alligators). We've lost the godly use of our homes.

Sadly many of us have transformed our homes into castles; we've removed our "Welcome" mat that used to be at the front door, and installed "Ring" doorbells so we can be alerted when someone walks up our sidewalk. Our fingers are poised over 911 as we watch strangers on our phones just in case they are hardened burglars who want to rob us blind.

You Have a Choice!

Notice Paul says, "and you want to go" (v. 27). We should jump at chances to have meals with unbelievers, especially at their invitation! But the Christian's desire does have a role to play. For what reason would a Christian not want to accept such an invitation? It might be that he or she knows it is a set-up to embarrass the believer on the issue of meats offered to idols. It's also possible that the unbeliever wants to argue about spiritual matters. And sometimes such conversations need to be conducted in private.

The question is: *Do you want to go?* For some of us, we know that we will feel uncomfortable in the home of someone still "far from God." My best pastoral advice to that kind of hesitancy is: "Grow up! Be uncomfortable! You've been invited to share a meal. So, go!'

Let Someone Else's Conscience Be Your Guide

Paul then instructs, "eat whatever is put before you without raising questions of conscience." Ignorance may not be bliss, but in this situation ignorance of where the meat came from is important. The believer is not to go with a list of conscience-driven restrictions. He or she is to eat whatever is put before them.

However, Paul writes, someone may say to you, "This has been offered in sacrifice." Paul advises, "then do not eat it, both for the sake of the one who told you and for the sake of conscience." (v. 28). But to whose conscience is Paul referring? He says in the next sentence, "I am referring to the other person's conscience, not yours." (v. 29). The implication seems to be that your conscience is clear in eating such meat. However, you are not the only person involved.

Paul then raises the question, "why is my freedom being judged by another's conscience?" But it is. That other person's conscience is enough to keep the believer from eating. Paul then writes, "If I take part in the meal with thankfulness, why am I denounced because of something I thank God for?" (v. 30).

Paul says that thankfulness should be sufficient to keep one from being denounced, but it often isn't. The bottom line for Paul is, "So whether you eat or drink or whatever you do, do it all for the glory of God." (v. 31).

However, we are not to cause anyone to stumble, "whether Jews, Greeks or the church of God" (v. 32). We are to "try to please everyone in every way." Why? Because, as Paul says, "For I am not seeking my own good but the good of many, so that they may be saved." (v. 33).

Is this text saying that, although eating meat offered to idols is nothing (because idols are nothing), we should abstain IF another's conscience believes it to be wrong? The conscience of someone other than yourself is the issue here. I am free to eat if I do it with thankfulness, but not if another's conscience is being offended.

Feelings

We introduced this chapter with the song lyrics of Debbie Boone's #1 single "You Light Up My Life." Although the song sounds like it is extolling romantic love, she said she was singing about God. As the daughter of the well-known Christian singer and actor Pat Boone, Debbie outraged Christians in 1977 when this song which included the words, "It can't be wrong when it feels so right." If the subject of the song was indeed God, I'm not sure how those words fit.

At any rate, many Jesus-followers took her song to mean, "Don't hesitate to do what your heart tells you to even if some other authority tells you it's wrong. Trust your feelings!"

We are not to compromise our morals regardless of how "it" feels. And being around those who are not yet in God's family will expose us to habits that we don't want to adopt. For some believers, they are deathly afraid they will be offered an alcoholic beverage. If your conscience forbids you from drinking, don't give a long sermon as to why you don't drink. Just ask for something else. It is highly unlikely that your unsaved friend is trying to get you intoxicated!

Some of my lost friends tell filthy stories and jokes. I don't walk away in disgust, shaking the dust off my sneakers, and pronounce curses on those who use the Lord's name in vain or tell dirty stories. I stay there and try to come up with the funniest clean story or joke when it's my turn to talk. My lost friends need to know that I love a good story or funny joke.[10]

All Things To All Men

The truth is, we are all uncomfortable around others who are not exactly like us. And the more seriously we take our Christian lives, the more distance there seems to be between us and those who need the Lord.

We need to be reminded that we have so much in common with those who are not yet believers in Jesus. We are both made in the image of God. We are both loved by Him. It may be that we both have families and children and grandchildren. We both have jobs and hobbies and skills and fears and dreams. *How have we Christians become so poor at finding contact points, points of commonality, with lost people?*

There is one more text we must examine before we conclude this chapter. And that text is I Corinthians 9 —

> 19 Though I am free and belong to no one, I have made myself a slave to everyone, to win as many as possible. 20 To the Jews I became like a Jew, to win the Jews. To those under the law I became like one under the law (though I myself am not under the law), so as to win those under the law. 21 To those not having the law I became like one not having the law (though I am not free from God's law but am under Christ's law), so as to win those not having the law. 22 To the weak I became weak, to win the weak. I have become all things to all people so that by all possible means I might save some. 23 I do all this for the sake of the gospel, that I may share in its blessings.

---

10 I have collected a beginning list of some of the best jokes I've found and I'll gladly send them to you if you email me (theoprof@bellsouth.net). Here are two email subscriptions (free) that you might want to join to get good material: https://gcfl.net/ ("The Good Clean Funnies List") and MikeysFunnies.com..

Getting Defensive

Before we think through these verses, let's examine the context of what Paul is saying. I Corinthians 9 presents Paul's defense of his apostleship. He testifies that he has seen the Lord and that the Corinthians themselves are the "seal of [his] apostleship" (v. 2).

He then speaks of certain rights that he has as an apostle. He has the right to food and drink. He has the right to take a believing wife. He has the right "to not work for a living" (vv. 3-6).

Paul then gives illustrations of how soldiers don't serve at their own expense. Those who plant vineyards are free to eat of their own grapes. One tending a flock has the right to drink the milk (v. 7). In fact, the Law itself says that we are not to "muzzle an ox while it is treading out the grain" (v. 9).

[Allow me a moment of frivolity. I've quoted (or rather misquoted) that saying to friends as "Do not *nuzzle* an ox while it is treading out the grain!" You know, it's never a good idea to nuzzle an ox!].

Paul makes it clear that God's concern is not oxen, but us! Because "whoever plows and threshes should be able to do so in the hope of sharing in the harvest" (v. 10). In short, Paul is making the case that the Corinthians are right to support him in his ministry and he is right to accept such support.

"But," Paul says, "we did not use this right." He says he would rather put up with anything than hinder the gospel of Christ (v. 12). The point is, *Paul exercised his right to give up his rights!* We then read about Paul's use of his freedom in verses 19-23.

As a free man, Paul consciously chose to make himself "a slave" to everyone, "to win as many as possible" (v. 19). He then specifies what he means. He became like a Jew to the Jews to win the Jews. He became like those under the law so as to win those under the law. To those not having the law (presumably the Gentiles) he became like one not having the law so to win those not having the law. To the weak he became weak. He concludes, "I have become all things to all people so that by all possible means I might save some" (v. 22).

What does this mean to us? It means that, although we are never to compromise the truth of the gospel, we have incredible freedom to use our talents and personalities to identify with and seek to win those outside the faith.

Can we talk? For many of us believers, our motto differs dramatically from Paul's. I believe it could be stated as, "I am willing to become a few things to a couple of people that one or two might just consider Jesus. But I don't really want to get too uncomfortable in the process!" Sometimes our happiness is at stake — and it needs to be nailed to the cross! If none of my relationships make me feel uncomfortable, I'm in trouble. I'm in this religion for the wrong reason. C.S. Lewis put it this way: "I didn't go to religion to make me happy. I always knew a bottle of Port would do that. If you want a religion to make you feel really comfortable, I certainly don't recommend Christianity."[11]

A Final Word about Compromise

Some compromises are neither right nor wrong. But the fear of compromising one's Christian convictions must not keep the believer from following His Lord's example of being a friend of sinners.

And we must come to grips with our own insatiable desire to protect our comfort at all costs. Living life with pagans will rattle our comfort cages to the core. But it's the right choice to make.

---

11 *God in the Dock* "Answers to Questions on Christianity." Part 1; Section 4; Question 1 (edited by Walter Hooper)

Questions for Chapter Six:

1.   Why don't we Christians get invited to more meals by our unsaved friends?

2.   We don't want to compromise the truths of the Christian faith. How can we practically deal with the fear of compromise and still develop deep relationships with lost people?

3.   How do we practically become "all things to all men"?

4.   How do we balance our Christianity with our place in our culture? Being anti-culture seems to get us nowhere. But becoming subsumed in our culture isn't the answer either. How would you define culture and advise a new believer about his or her place in it?

CHAPTER SEVEN:

"WE'VE A STORY TO TELL TO THE NATIONS" ♫
(Traditional Missions Song)

"There is no greater agony than bearing an untold story inside you." (Maya Angelou)

"One of the most valuable things we can do to heal one another is to listen to each other's stories." (Rebecca Falls)

"I like to listen. I have learned a great deal from listening carefully. Most people never listen." (Ernest Hemingway)

"Would you like to come over for coffee sometime? I've got some questions I want to ask you." My friend Michael invited me over to his home and I went that afternoon. He and I have played a lot of tennis together and he knows that I'm a follower of Jesus.

The questions he had for me had to do with someone asking him about his nationality. He has a bit of an accent and was offended that someone wanted to know where he was from. I suggested that the question seemed to be a fairly innocent one and we talked for a while about whether he should be upset. I gave him my best advice and said that people down South can be a bit nosey and that the person probably didn't mean anything negative by the question.

A Different Accent

The next thing I knew, Michael was asking me about different world religions! I hadn't brought up the issue of religion. He did. We talked for over two hours at his kitchen table, drinking coffee, and debating the various positive and negative features of Buddhism, Islam, and Christianity. I was able to share the gospel with him — and our friendship continues. In fact, I'm having lunch with him today.

Just came back from lunch with my friend Michael. We talked about his recent health issues, his improved cholesterol numbers, his triglycerides, and . . . death. Really. He's had some heart problems and said he's not afraid to die, but fears how his nine-year-old daughter would cope with it. I let him talk. I'm thankful he's doing better health-wise. I did say, "Maybe we should fear death — unless we're sure we're right with God." But he kind of passed over that and changed subjects. But we had lunch together. And he even had me give thanks before we ate lunch!

I'm convinced if you and I are to be a friend of sinners, we will need to have many conversations about a lot of things. And we will need to be prepared to do some heavy *listening!*

Learning to Listen

One of my all-time favorite singers is Ray Charles. He lost his eyesight as a child and once said, "Most people take their hearing for granted. I can't. My eyes are my handicap, but my ears are my opportunity. My ears show me what my eyes can't. My ears tell me 99 percent of what I need to know about my world."[12]

Listening to another person's story demands one's attention. I'm convinced that many, many people would love to have someone show interest in their lives and would gladly begin to share some of their stories — if only someone would listen.

If I seriously want to be a friend of sinners, like Jesus was, I need to be willing to listen to their stories. Here are some steps that are helping me grow in this area.

(1) Begin with Prayer

I know. I know. Christians think prayer is the answer for everything. Well, when it comes to listening, praying before meeting with your lost friend will calibrate your mind to be alert and ready if spiritual matters come up. Asking the Lord to calm your heart

---

12 Here's another quote from Ray Charles that Christians would have a hard time affirming: "I'm a firm believer in God himself, but that's as far as I can go. I'm not any denomination. I'm not Catholic or Presbyterian or Baptist or Methodist or Jewish or Muslim. I'm none of those things. And I'm sure that's just fine with God." https://www.brainyquote.com/quotes/ray_charles_655344

and prepare you for whatever conversation takes place is critical. I agree with E.M. Bounds who said, "Talking to men for God is a great thing, but talking to God for men is greater still."

Let's get specific in our praying. As John Wesley put it, "Prayer is where the action is!" Instead of praying, "Lord, please save my friend Bill," how about praying, "Lord, make me attentive to what Bill shares with me. Help me not to push spiritual things too hard on him. Father, give me ears to hear what he is really saying." Ask the Lord for wisdom in your conversation. And, if at all possible, don't be the one to conclude your time together. Let him or her end the meeting.

(2) Let Your Friend Set the Agenda

True friendship involves letting the other person set the agenda for the conversation. Developing a relationship requires that we give our utmost attention to the other person. Trust God to work through your presence in listening and listening hard to their issues or statements.

Too often Christians have been guilty of having a kind of script when a conversation with an unsaved person begins. We've been known to manipulate our talks with another person, "guiding" the conversation to something more "spiritual." Lost people aren't stupid. No one appreciates being a kind of project whose words and thoughts are hijacked in a direction they don't want to go.

One of the many part-time jobs that I've had in my life was being a Time/Life telemarketer. Okay, put down your rocks. I know it's an intrusive and cruel way to make a living. But it was all I had. And I had a script. My script would answer almost any objection someone had to joining our book subscription. "Your cat's tail is caught in the front door? Our books will give you the history of the domestication of felines (after you've put ointment on your scratches)." "You think you're having a heart attack? Our medical series will give you specific questions to ask — if you're still conscious." [I didn't last at that job too long. And, after getting fired, went home and took a long shower].

Can we all agree to put our phone numbers on the Do Not Call list? [A number of years ago I was much more spiritual and made a promise to the Lord. My promise was this: "Lord, for the next month whenever a telemarketer calls me, I will share the gospel with them." I kept my promise. Whenever I got a call, I would say something like this: "I appreciate the product you're trying to sell me, but I'm not interested right now. By the way, I made a promise to God a while back that might interest you. Would you like to hear it?" I had some claim to be Christians; one said he *was* God; and *several* simply hung up on *me*!]. Nowadays we receive robotic calls — and there is no salvation for robots. [I got a call the other day and suspected it was a robotic call. I said, "Martha, are you a human?" The robot laughed and said, "Of course!" I then said, "Martha, what is 2 plus 2?" She did not answer. Before the robot hung up on me, I said, "Martha, you lied to me. And that was not very nice."]

Treat the other person . . . as a *person!* They are not a project. They are not an "assignment." They are someone made in the image of God who is a sinner by nature and by practice — and they need the good news of the gospel. You're not a telemarketer or a timeshare sales person. Don't act like one.

(3) Don't Give Partial Attention

Our present culture thinks it can do several things at once, but that's a myth. All we wind up doing is giving partial attention to multiple objects and often end up doing poorly at each of them. I remember having lunch with a seminary colleague. We were to plan a chapel message that we would give together. During our entire lunch he was checking his cell phone. Now, to be honest, he was the pastor of two churches. But, as far as I knew, he was not waiting for a call about a church member in critical care in the hospital. He was just checking his email. And I felt like chopped liver. [I've never quite understood the expression "I feel like chopped liver." I hate liver. And I guess it's even worse when it's chopped.]

Linda Stone coined the term "Continuous Partial Attention" in 1998. The idea is paying simultaneous attention to a number of sources of incoming information, but at a superficial level. As one writer says, "It usually involves skimming the surface of the incoming data, picking out the relevant details, and moving on to the next stream. You're paying attention, but only partially. That lets you cast a wider net, but it also runs the risk of keeping you from really studying the fish."

Some would say that our age, often called the "Information Age," has devolved into the "Age of Interruption." One writer puts it this way: "People are constantly interrupted by emails, spam, instant messages and cellphones, making attention a scarce resource in this era." Continuous partial attention produces more stress in the brain and inhibits contemplation and thoughtful decisions. It will dilute our efforts to focus on the person in front of us, will lower productivity levels, lead to over-stimulation, and ultimately result in a lack of fulfillment.[13]

Some scholars differentiate between Continuous Partial Attention and multitasking. But in a general sense, they are quite similar. And only giving partial attention to the person in front of you is rude and counter-productive to a healthy relationship.

I heard one person say, "I'm multitasking: I can listen, ignore and forget at the same time." Another person quipped, ""My brain is like an internet browser: I have 17 tabs open, four of them are frozen, and I've no idea where the music is coming from"…

Someone named Bosco Tjan put it this way: "Most of the time multitasking is an illusion. You think you are multitasking, but in reality you're actually wasting time switching from one task to another." Focus on the person in front of you.

---

13   https://en.wikipedia.org/wiki/Continuous_partial_attention

(4) Remember the Details

If you are listening hard to your unsaved friend, there will be some issues or important events that might be mentioned that you should remember. Remembering means you were listening hard and you care! Write things down. That's what friends do. They don't just hear what's said; they really listen . . . and remember.

We don't want to just go through the motions of listening. We want to *learn* about the other person. We want to grow in our understanding of their life and where the Christian gospel might find a foothold in their thinking. But if I don't remember details of a conversation ("Does Sarah have two children . . . or three?"), the message I am communicating is: "I'm not all that interested in the specifics of your life. Just let me get out my message to you."

Technology can really help us here. We can use our phones to text someone about an event they told us about. Actually using our phones to *call someone* (shocker!) to see how their surgery went or just to say we were thinking of them are wise choices we can make.

(5) Keep Confidences

It is critical that you show yourself trustworthy. As your lost friends begin to share some of their deepest disappointments, challenges, and heartaches, you will need to guard that information.

Both my wife and my daughter are trained counselors. My daughter is a licensed clinical therapist and music therapist. My wife is a guidance counselor and professional plan facilitator for learning-challenged students. So I'm covered. Whether my problems are musical or guidance or clinical or challenging, my wife and my daughter can help me.

As we develop friendships with lost people, we are not to become therapists. But there are some similarities between deep friendships and counseling. As one therapist put it, "Always remember that for each patient you see you may be the only person in their life capable of both hearing and holding their pain. If that isn't sacred, I don't know what is."

We are indeed on a sacred mission. And we don't know what circumstances will lead our lost friend to consider the gospel. But we can hear — and hold — their pain and trust God to put His divine finger on that area of need.

By the way, we can — and should — ask our churches to pray for our developing relationships with those who need the Lord. But we don't have to give details. We don't have to say, "My friend Fred is going through a messy divorce right now." What if Fred shows up at one of your church services and someone asks him, "You're Fred, right? I'm sorry to hear about your divorce. . . ." Trust can be irrevocably broken, can't it?

(6) Be Vulnerable or Transparent

One of the greatest barriers to friendships with lost people is the myth that Christians are perfect. Don't be afraid to share some of your struggles with your friend. This is exactly where you might bring the Lord in. The writer Madeleine L'Engle puts it this way: "When we were children, we used to think that when we were grown-up we would no longer be vulnerable. But to grow up is to accept vulnerability. . . . To be alive is to be vulnerable."

Christians fail in many ways. We fail the Lord. We fail each other. We fail ourselves in not becoming more the people God wants us to be. Why do we not share some of those failures with others? More specifically, with our lost friends? What are we afraid of? Our weaknesses and struggles make the Lord more, not less, real! Unless we've swallowed the myth that we're perfect. I love the statement that says that one of the greatest things about being a Christian is that I no longer have to defend my own goodness. When we share our mistakes, we are able to model before our lost friends our honest confession, genuine sorrow, and biblical hope for our moving on in the Christian life.

"Vulnerability is a magnet for honesty," says Dr. Salma Farook, "and honesty is the very basis of human connections." The Christian life, above almost anything else, is honest and practical. We can afford to be honest because the Lord is still working on us. And being a follower of Jesus is immensely practical. God's Word and God's Spirit help us to grow and face our challenges with courage.

In his book on George Washington entitled *His Excellency: George Washington*, Joseph Ellise makes the comment, "Because he could not afford to fail, he could not afford to trust." We know that we fail. And we can afford to trust, even our unsaved friends, with the truth of our failures.

Identification or Imagination?

As your unsaved friend begins to share some of his or her struggles, you have the opportunity to connect. You can sympathize with their struggle in one of two ways. If you've gone through the same trial, you can identify with their issue. For example, if they are being challenged by a rebellious son or daughter — and you have as well — you can say, "I can certainly identify with what you are going through. Let me tell you about our child . . ."

If they share with you something that you have not gone through, you might use imagination. For example, you might say something like, "Wow. That sounds like a tough thing to be going through right now. I can imagine that you might be worrying yourself silly . . ."

Identification or imagination can both be ways that we can connect with other human beings who are experiencing challenges in life. We want to bridge the gap between Christians (who aren't perfect) and those not yet in God's family who need our friendship.

(7) Commit to Long-Term Relationships

Relationships can be long-term or short-term. Pastor John MacArthur tells about how he was on a flight somewhere and the person in the seat next to him asked him what he did for a living. He said, "I tell people how they can have their sins forgiven. Interested?" He says the person got up, went to the back of the airplane, and MacArthur never saw him again.

Some connections are brief. But the burden of this book is to challenge us not to brief encounters but to developing relationships that will be, optimally, life-long. We have no right to spiritually blackmail people with words like the following: "Listen. I'll be your friend for the next six months. If you don't trust Christ by then, I'm moving on to someone else!" Certainly we would never say something like that to another person, but we might find ourselves treating lost people that way.

Instead we ought to live in such a way that our process could be described somewhat as follows: "Listen. I'm thankful for your friendship. And I promise: My relationship to you does not depend on what you do with Jesus. I very much want you to come to know Him, but I'll be your friend for life. And if you're on your deathbed before I'm on mine, I will be there, by your side, telling you again of the Lord's love for you. Deal?"

I'm not sure most of us are committed to this kind of life-long relationships. Granted, the Lord Jesus, in a sense, isn't our example here because of the brevity of His earthly life. But I don't get the impression from reading the gospels that He ended connections with sinners because they didn't believe. The story of the rich young ruler (which we looked at in Chapter Five) culminated in his walking away from Jesus "because he had great riches" (Luke 18:23). Jesus did not chase him down the road to renegotiate the terms of salvation with him. He let him walk away.

Let's face it: Some of our non-Christian friends will sever their ties with us. Yes, we are told in 2 Corinthians 6 that light has no fellowship with darkness. But our theme throughout this book isn't that we should seek spiritual friendship with those who don't know Christ. Some may tire of our Christian testimony, but none should walk away because they felt we were not invested, long-term, in a relationship with them.

Jesus indeed spoke about not casting our pearls before swine in Matthew 7. Let's look briefly at that text:

> "Do not judge, or you too will be judged. 2 For in
> the same way you judge others, you will be judged, and

with the measure you use, it will be measured to you. 3 "Why do you look at the speck of sawdust in your brother's eye and pay no attention to the plank in your own eye? 4 How can you say to your brother, 'Let me take the speck out of your eye,' when all the time there is a plank in your own eye? 5 You hypocrite, first take the plank out of your own eye, and then you will see clearly to remove the speck from your brother's eye. 6 "Do not give dogs what is sacred; do not throw your pearls to pigs. If you do, they may trample them under their feet, and turn and tear you to pieces. 7 "Ask and it will be given to you; seek and you will find; knock and the door will be opened to you. 8 For everyone who asks receives; the one who seeks finds; and to the one who knocks, the door will be opened.

Please notice several observations about this text. First, the not-throwing-your-pearls-before-pigs occurs in the passage that tells us not to judge hypocritically. Matthew 7 is often misunderstood as teaching that we are not to judge at all. Some might say, "Verse 1 says clearly, 'Do not judge, or you will be judged.' So," they conclude, "we shouldn't judge!"

The problem is that they haven't read far enough. Matthew 7 (verses 1-5) is about judging *hypocritically.* Jesus is saying that we dare not use one standard to judge ourselves and a much higher standard to judge others. The same measure will be used against us (v. 2) as we use to judge others.

In fact, Jesus is teaching that proper judgment begins with our getting the plank out of our own eye so that we can "then see clearly to remove the speck from [our] brother's eye" (v. 5). Our own plank obscures our vision — of our own sin and perhaps of the sins of others. But we are clearly told to remove the speck from our brother's eye.

We then read about not giving to dogs what is sacred and not throwing our pearls to pigs (v. 6). It seems that today in the States people virtually worship their dogs. Have you seen the bumper stickers lately that say things like, "My dog makes me happy. You, not so much." Or the sticker that says "Dog Dad." Or the one that says "I love my Grandog." My favorite is the one that says, "My therapist has a wet nose."

People today treat dogs better than their children. But people are more important than dogs. And we don't give what is sacred to dogs!

Nor do we throw our pearls to pigs. I'm not sure why anyone is throwing pearls at all, but the point is that pigs won't appreciate the pearls. They won't value them. Jesus then says, "If you do, they may trample them under their feet, and turn and tear you to pieces."

Large pigs are dangerous. I was once invited to a hunting club to help rid the property of wild hogs who were ruining the land for the deer. The pigs were enormous (200-300 pounds). And we were warned that wild pigs can charge a hunter and inflict serious injury.

Fortunately I didn't have any encounter with the swine, but a friend shot two of them (each weighing about 250 pounds). [I felt like giving him a pearl necklace to commemorate the occasion, but, hey, it was another guy!]

By the way, did you notice that the next two verses (vv. 7-8) talk about those who are seeking the Lord? This might help us understand verse 6. Perhaps the thought is that those who mock and ridicule and reject the gospel of Jesus should not be catered to. To those who appear not to have any interest in the gospel, in fact who may attack the gospel at every point, we might want to say, "Listen. I'm not going to discuss or argue spiritual matters with you at this time. I'm not sure you are really seeking to know God. But, if you should ever come to the point when you really want to know how to get into God's family, you call me. 24/7."

Summary

What has been our burden in this chapter? Yes, we've a story to tell to the nations . . . and to our neighbors. But before we can tell our story to our neighbors, we need to do some listening to *their* stories. And as we share our common human stories with one another, as one writer puts it, we might well see that "your story could be the key that unlocks someone else's prison. Don't be afraid to share it."

There's a relief in knowing that I can listen to any story my lost friend tells me — and I don't have to be the answer man for him or her. I can give my undivided attention to their struggle, affirm to them my concern for them, and put that situation in the Lord's hands. I don't have to preach a sermon or dive into in-depth counseling. As Rachel Naomi Remen, clinical professor of family and community medicine at the University of California at San Francisco School of Medicine, states so eloquently, "The most basic and powerful way to connect to another person is to listen. Just listen. Perhaps the most important thing we ever give each other is our attention . . . A loving silence often has far more power to heal and to connect than the most well-intentioned words."[14]

We've got stories to listen to! And to be an excellent listener involves critical elements such as beginning with prayer, letting the other person set the agenda, refusing to give only partial attention, remembering what is shared with us, proving ourselves trustworthy, being vulnerable, and committing ourselves to long-term relationships.

---

14 http://cultureofempathy.com/References/Experts/Others/Rachel-Naomi-Remen.htm

Questions for Chapter Seven:

1. Would you describe yourself as a good listener? Why or why not?

2. We give seven principles that may help us become better listeners. Which principle will require the most effort from you, do you think?

3. How can we commit ourselves to long-term relationships with unbelievers and yet not seek to somehow have spiritual fellowship with them?

CHAPTER EIGHT:

"Let's Get Lost (in Each Other's Arms)" ♫

(Chet Baker)

"You're never truly lost if someone cares enough to come find you. Lost is waiting to be found." (Barbara Claypole White, *Echoes of Family*)

"Not every lost soul wants to be found, because not every lost [soul] is lost; some of them found something or many thing[s] or even everything in their lostness!" (Mehmet Murat ildan)

Daniel Boone was once asked if he had ever gotten lost. He said, "No, but I was bewildered for three days once."

"We have in a real sense lost sense of the lostness of the lost." (Dr. Francis Schaeffer)

Many years ago a little boy and his twin sister went missing in a small community outside Boston. After they were gone for several hours, the police were called and a search party was organized. Meanwhile, the little boy and girl both showed up when they heard the commotion as the search party started their work. They asked what was going on and were told that a little boy and girl had been lost. For the next two hours they helped search for themselves!

Getting Lost

But people don't search for themselves when they are lost. The BBC had an internet article entitled "Your Stories of Getting Lost." It began with the sentence: "Here are some of the best reader tales that describe the sense of adventure, survival and amusement that can come out of getting lost." Some travel magazines talk about the joy of getting lost in some of the most beautiful cities in the world. One writer said, "There is value to be found in losing our way every once in a while." Another person described his adventure of getting lost. He says, "I walked into the jungle in Siem Reap (Cambodia) following the sound of macaws and ended up surrounded by land-mine warning signs!"

On a personal note, I don't know what I would do without the GPS feature on my phone. I'm terrible with directions. I tell my wife about my getting lost or going the wrong way or not knowing whether to turn left or right at an intersection.

She says, "Well, take the direction you think of first, and do the opposite!" That sounds reasonable, but at my age I forget whether I thought of left or right first. And so I sit at the intersection confused and close to tears.

Once she was in the car and she said we had to turn around and go the other way. I backed into a driveway, pulled out, and began heading in the same direction we had been going. She just laughed and said, "Let's try that one more time."

When it comes to *spiritual* lostness, the Bible is clear that such lostness is lethal and not a lark. True, life might present some adventure and amusement for those outside Christ, but the reality is there is a real God and there will be a real judgment. Let's think about some of the biblical descriptions of man's natural condition of lostness.

Won't Stand in the Judgment

We read of the wicked in Psalm 1 that they "will not stand in the judgment" (v. 5). The point is not that the wicked will not *appear* before God's judgment, but that they will not *survive* His judgment. The Hebrew word means to "maintain oneself." One commentator says: "When they come to be judged, they shall be condemned. They shall have nothing to plead in their behalf." (Adam Clarke's Commentary). We read in Revelation 6:17, "For the great day of his wrath is come; and who shall be able to stand?" I Peter 4:18 says, "If the righteous scarcely be saved, where shall the ungodly and sinner appear?" When the opportunity presents itself, we might say something like this to our unsaved friend who questions the possibility of God's judgment: "You will stand before God's judgment even if you don't think you will."

If you study Psalm 1 — and I highly recommend that you do — you will find that all of humanity is divided into two and only two categories: the blessed man who knows God and the wicked who will not survive God's judgment. Those two categories are consistently traced throughout the Bible. What are some other descriptions of the lost person's condition before God?

Already Condemned

We read in God's Word that the condemnation of the wicked has already been pronounced. John 3:18 says, "Whoever believes in him is not condemned, but whoever does not believe stands condemned already because they have not believed in the name of God's one and only Son." Already condemned.

Many people think that the verdict of condemnation or pardon will be decided only at the final judgment seat of God. They envision a massive bronze scale which is filled with our good deeds in one tray and our bad deeds in the other tray. The imagery, of course, is not biblical, for no one can be saved by their good deeds. But if that picture were true, according to the Bible the good deeds' tray would be empty, and the sheer gravity of our sins would cause the bad deeds' tray to loudly crash overloaded to the ground, for Scripture says that all our good works are like filthy rags before God.

By the way, the expression "filthy rags" (Isaiah 64:6) is quite fascinating. The "term 'filthy rags' is very strong. The word filthy is a translation of the Hebrew word '*iddah*', which literally means 'the bodily fluids from a woman's menstrual cycle.' The word rags is a translation of '*begged*', meaning 'a rag or garment.' Therefore, these 'righteous acts' are considered by God as repugnant as a soiled feminine hygiene product."[15]

The Bible teaches that even before death the sinner is already condemned. Only belief or trust in Jesus Christ removes God's wrath from that person. Of course there will be a end-of-time

---

15   https://www.gotquestions.org/filthy-rags.html

judgment, but there God's eternal and irrevocable verdict will be finally announced. We read the following in Revelation 20:

> 11 Then I saw a great white throne and him who was seated on it. The earth and the heavens fled from his presence, and there was no place for them. 12 And I saw the dead, great and small, standing before the throne, and books were opened. Another book was opened, which is the book of life. The dead were judged according to what they had done as recorded in the books. 13 The sea gave up the dead that were in it, and death and Hades gave up the dead that were in them, and each person was judged according to what they had done. 14 Then death and Hades were thrown into the lake of fire. The lake of fire is the second death. 15 Anyone whose name was not found written in the book of life was thrown into the lake of fire.

We learn here in Revelation that there will be a great white throne at the end of time. All the dead, small and great, will stand before God's throne. Several books will be opened and the dead will be judged by their works as recorded in the books (v. 12). The sea, death, and Hades will give up the dead in them and each person will be judged according to what they had done (v. 13).

So the dead will be shown by their own deeds that they do not somehow merit heaven. Death and Hades will be thrown into the lake of fire (the second death) (v. 14). We then read that "Anyone whose name was not found written in the book of life was thrown into the lake of fire" (v. 15).

One may answer, when asked if hell is eternal, "No, but the lake of fire is." This text teaches us that all people will be judged — and those whose names aren't in the book of life will suffer the same fate as the false prophet, the beast, and the devil (see Revelation 20:7-10).

Under God's Wrath

John 3 says, "Whoever believes in the Son has eternal life, but whoever rejects[16] the Son will not see life, for God's wrath remains on them" (v. 36). God's wrath "remains on them." They are already under the wrath of God.

When you talk to your lost friend, don't you wish that you could be blatantly honest and say something like this: "You know, my friend, that God loves you. You know that God gave His Son for your sins. But the bad news of the good news is that you are not in a spiritually neutral condition. Until you trust Christ as your Savior, the wrath of God is presently on you. The only way to extricate yourself from under His wrath is to believe the gospel."

A Brief Excursus

Do you remember studying Jonathan Edwards' sermon "Sinners in the Hands of an Angry God" in high school? The study of the wrath of God by this eighteenth century preacher and scholar contains some strong statements on God's wrath. Here are a few examples:

Emphasizing the urgency of repentance, Edwards uses a variety of expressions to point out the certainty of God's judgment of the sinner. He declares that "there is nothing that keeps wicked men at any one moment out of hell, but the mere pleasure of God." Com-

---

16 Neal Punt in his book *A Theology of Inclusivism* suggests that no one is actually condemned until they *consciously* reject the gospel. He says, Christians believe and agree that personal acceptance of Christ is necessary in those places and periods of time in which the name of Christ is actually accessible, but what about those places and periods of time in which one could not learn of our Saviour because His Name was inaccessible? . . . we should move from an 'All persons will finally be lost except those who the Bible declares will be saved' position to an 'All persons will be saved except those who the Bible declares will be finally lost' position, thereby regaining the overall more positive approach of the earliest fathers of the Church. http://www.ukapologetics.net/08/puntbookreview.htm Based our on discussion in this chapter, would you agree or disagree with Punt?

bining several word pictures, he says of the wicked that "the wrath of God burns against them, their damnation does not slumber; the pit is prepared, the fire is made ready, the furnace is now hot, ready to receive them; the flames do now rage and glow. The glittering sword is whet, and held over them, and the pit hath opened its mouth under them."

In fact, Edwards describes the state of the man without Christ as liable to self-combustion: "There are in the souls of wicked men those hellish principles reigning, that would presently kindle and flame out into hell fire, if it were not for God's restraints. There is laid in the very nature of carnal men, a foundation for the torments of hell." Man's own nature is composed of "the seeds of hell fire." Edwards mixes this concept of the wicked's virtual combustibility with the scene of a satanic welcoming party: "the devil is waiting for them, hell is gaping for them, the flames gather and flash about them, and would fain lay hold on them, and swallow them up; the fire bent up in their own hearts is struggling to break out."

Later in his sermon Edwards focuses upon the sheer gravity of man's own sin: "Your wickedness makes you as it were heavy as lead, and to tend downwards with great weight and pressure towards hell; and if God should let you go, you would immediately sink and swiftly descend and plunge into the bottomless gulf."

"You cannot save yourself," Edwards warns, "your own care and all your righteousness, would have no more influence to uphold you and keep you out of hell, than a spider's web would have to stop a fallen rock." Describing God's wrath as a dreadful storm, as dam waters that can no longer be held back, and as a flood of God's vengeance, he then takes up a hunting image: "The bow of God's wrath is bent," he says, "and the arrow made ready on the string, and justice bends the arrow at your heart, and strains the bow, and it is nothing but the mere pleasure of God, and that of an angry God, without any promise or obligation at all, that keeps the arrow one moment from being made drunk with your blood."

Edwards goes so far as to describe the Christless sinner as an object of God's hatred: "The God who holds you over the pit of hell, much as one holds a spider, or some loathsome insect over the fire, abhors you, and is dreadfully provoked . . . . you are ten thousand times more abominable in His eyes, than the most hateful venomous serpent is in ours."

Some might object, "I thought God *loved* us!?" Yes, the Bible does teach the love of God. But it also teaches God's holy hatred and righteous wrath against sin and sinners. The scholar John Calvin struggled with these two, apparently contradictory, truths. He concluded, "God loved me even when He hated me."

Returning to the idea of God's "mere" mercy, Edwards says to this Connecticut congregation in 1741: "It is to be ascribed to nothing else, that you did not go to hell the last night; that you was [sic] suffered to awake again in this world, after you closed your eyes to sleep. And there is no other reason to be given, why you have not dropped into hell since you arose in the morning, but that God's hand has held you up."[17]

Don't let your high school English teacher's twisted interpretation of Edwards' sermon ruin it for you. We need to think about God's wrath — a theme often referred to in the Word of God.[18]

Enemies of God

The Bible is brutally honest about our condition before we trust Christ. We read in Romans 5:10, "For if, while we were God's enemies, we were reconciled to him through the death of his Son, how much more, having been reconciled, shall we be saved through his life!" Paul has already said in Romans 5 that Christ died for the ungodly, for us, "when we were still powerless" (v. 6). We were not righteous people who merited Christ's death for us. We read, "But

---

17 I've examined Edwards' sermon in my book *The Other Side of the Good News: Confronting Contemporary Challenges to Jesus' Teaching on Hell* (Christian Focus, 2003).

18 An article on God's wrath I wrote is entitled "Warning a Wrath-Deserving World: Evangelicals and the Overhaul of Hell" which may be found at http://apprising.org/2011/07/08/warning-a-wrath-deserving-world-evangelicals-and-the-overhaul-of-hell/

God demonstrates his own love for us in this: While we were still sinners, Christ died for us." (v. 8).

Scripture is clear about our status before conversion. We read the following in Ephesians 2:

> As for you, you were dead in your transgressions and sins, 2 in which you used to live when you followed the ways of this world and of the ruler of the kingdom of the air, the spirit who is now at work in those who are disobedient. 3 All of us also lived among them at one time, gratifying the cravings of our flesh and following its desires and thoughts. Like the rest, we were by nature deserving of wrath. 4 But because of his great love for us, God, who is rich in mercy, 5 made us alive with Christ even when we were dead in transgressions—it is by grace you have been saved. 6 And God raised us up with Christ and seated us with him in the heavenly realms in Christ Jesus, 7 in order that in the coming ages he might show the incomparable riches of his grace, expressed in his kindness to us in Christ Jesus. 8 For it is by grace you have been saved, through faith—and this is not from yourselves, it is the gift of God— 9 not by works, so that no one can boast. 10 For we are God's handiwork, created in Christ Jesus to do good works, which God prepared in advance for us to do.

There is incredible language used in this text. Paul deals with two themes in these verses: (1) Our B.C. (Before Conversion) Condition (vv. 1-3) and (2) Our A.C. (After Conversion) Condition (vv. 4-10).

Our B.C. Condition

Notice some of the language used about our before conversion condition. Paul says the Ephesians (and we) were "dead in [our] transgressions and sins" (v. 1). Spiritually dead. But he goes on and says "in which you used to live" (v. 2). I can't help it, but the only term that comes to my mind is a spiritual zombie! We were dead but used to live in those transgressions and sins.

Not only did we live in those things, but we were followers of "the ways of the world and of the ruler of the kingdom of the air" (v. 2). We were not alone in our rebellion, but became followers of the original Rebel. This other personality encourages and facilitates us living our lives against God — and he is none other than the devil himself! He is "the spirit who is now at work in those who are disobedient" (v. 2).

We also had additional human company. We are told that we "lived among them at one time" (v. 3). Who's the "them"? Obviously the ones "who are disobedient" (v. 2). We belonged to the community of the condemned, wayward souls who seek to gratify "the cravings of our flesh and [to follow] its desires and thoughts" (v. 3).

What a package! We were spiritual zombies who followed the devil and all those disobedient ones who without restraint craved their own desires and thoughts. Paul concludes this horrifying section about our B.C. condition by saying, "like the rest, we were by nature deserving of wrath" (v. 3).[19] Wow! But let's notice the After Conversion statements in this passage:

Our A.C. Condition

In verses 4-10 we learn of our after conversion condition. God's motivation to save us was "his great love," his being "rich in mercy," 'the incomparable riches of his grace," and his "kindness." What did He do for us? We learn that He "made us alive with Christ" and saved us by His grace (v. 5).

We are also told that He has "raised us up with Christ" and has "seated us with him in the heavenly realms in Christ Jesus" (v. 6). We then learn that we can be a kind of display case of "the incomparable riches of his grace" (v. 7).

---

19 Ephesians 2 continues and describes the Gentile before conversion as "separate from Christ, excluded from citizenship in Israel and foreigners to the covenants of the promise, without hope and without God in the world. " (v. 12)

We are saved by grace, not by our works, so that all the glory goes to the Lord and none goes to us (vv. 8-9). But our after-conversion works are important. As God's "handiwork" we are to get busy — and do good deeds which God has prepared in advance for us to do (v. 10).

Why So Negative?

One might ask, why have we gone to so much trouble to show that before conversion the lost person is already condemned, under God's wrath, and an enemy of God who won't survive God's judgment? Well, we are actually appealing to two audiences.

First, I'm not persuaded that Christians are convinced that lost people are truly . . . lost. They are around fairly decent folk all day and find it difficult to believe that such co-workers or neighbors or friends will be separated from God forever. Theirs is a theology of an optimistic heart instead of one resting on the clear Word of God. Do you and I honestly look at each person we come in contact with every day and think, "I wonder if this person is 'still in their sins' (i.e., in an unsaved condition)"? Christians need to be awakened from the Satanic spell that everything is going to be pretty much okay with everybody at the end of time. Dr. Francis Schaeffer's challenge bears repeating, "We have in a real sense lost sense of the lostness of the lost."[20]

Second, at some point in our developing relationships with lost people, we are going to have to bring up the biblical truths of man's lostness in his or her sins. To paraphrase C.S. Lewis, we "have need of the strongest spell that can be found to wake us from the evil enchantment of" universalistic optimism that everything

---

20 William Paul Young, author of the popular book *The Shack*, clearly identifies himself as a universalist (one who believes that no one will finally be lost). In his book *Lies We Believe about God* Young writes, "God does not wait for my choice and then 'save me.' God has acted decisively and universally for all humankind. Now our daily choice is to either grow and participate in *that* reality or continue to live in the blindness of our own independence. Are you suggesting that everyone is saved? That you believe in universal salvation? That is exactly what I am saying." (p. 118).

will be okay with everybody. Our unsaved friends need to hear the truths of God's holiness and our sinfulness.

Helping People Get Lost

One preacher put it this way, "Before people can get saved, they have to get lost!"

Hardly does the average person think of themselves as lost. Flawed, maybe. Certainly not perfect. But LOST? And many are convinced of two clear "facts": (1) God is too loving to condemn anyone (especially them) for eternity. And (2) their sin or sins aren't bad enough to imprison them in hell forever. "What kind of sick theology teaches eternal lostness?", they might ask. Here are a few steps we can take on this quest of helping lost people realize their lostness.

(1) Speak Autobiographically

When we talk about lostness we need to talk about ourselves first. We need to describe what we've learned about our own lostness and how God in His mercy led us to repentance and faith. It seems to me that every conversion story ought to have at least an element of desperation, a realization that we deserved not God's love, but His judgment.

If we speak only of God's love, some will inwardly respond, "Of course, God loves me. That's great!" But that's not the whole gospel. For those who don't believe, they remain under God's wrath. And don't go pointing fingers at others. Point at yourself and how God in His grace saved you from His righteous anger.

(2) Correct Poor Theology

We may need to correct faulty ideas about God and man. What we mean is that many have little to no concept of God's holiness and hatred of sin. As someone once said, "God is allergic to sin." We need to see ourselves as sinners in need of a Savior.

This is one reason why long-term friendships with lost people are critical. We must give them time to think about their own sin, their sense of guilt, their longing for forgiveness.

Let me emphasize that the New Testament, especially the book of Acts, demonstrates a fascinating cooperation between the witnessing believer and God the Holy Spirit. As I read Acts, believers worked diligently to give evidences for the Messiahship and deity of the Lord Jesus. They spent time and debated with Jews, Gentiles, philosophers, and the intellectual curious of the day (see Paul in Acts 17). Our job is to convince the unbeliever of the truth of the gospel.

The Holy Spirit's job is to bring conviction of sin to the unbeliever's heart. That's not our job. And we should diligently pray for that internal ministry of the Spirit, that He would bless and use our words and lives to arouse a sense of guilt in our lost friends.[21]

(3) Be Open to Their Questions

When our friends get to know us, and trust us, they will begin to ask us questions. We need to be prepared to answer them. And if we don't have a ready answer, we should say something like the following: "That's a terrific question. Would you give me a couple of days to do a bit of research on that issue?"

One of the questions that I've been asked is, "I can see that you're really into religion, huh?" A simple response that I've heard is the following: "No, not really. You see, I spell 'religion' D O." "D O?" "Yes, religion is about what you DO. How many good works you do. But the problem with religion is you don't know what the quota is. How do you know when you've done enough good things?" "Huh. I never thought of it that way," your friend says. You continue: "I'm into Christianity. And 'Christianity' is spelled D O N E." "Done?" "Yes, Jesus did for us what we could not do for ourselves."

---

21   The late R.C. Sproul's classic series on "The Holiness of God" is quite helpful here.

(4) Ask Them Good Questions

As we get to know our non-Christian friends, they may become more open to our questions. We might ask them, if they profess to be religious, something like the following: "Would you say you are a Christian?" They might say, "Well, yes, I am." "May I ask you a question?" "Of course." "Would you describe yourself as a 'cultural Christian' or a 'biblical Christian?' "I don't understand," they might say. "What's a 'cultural Christian'?" You might respond, "A cultural Christian is someone who affirms the existence of God, attends church once in a while, tries to live by the Golden Rule, is kind to his neighbors. That sort of thing." "Oh, I guess that pretty much describes me," they might say. "But what is a 'biblical Christian'?" You might say, "I'm glad you asked." Then you can tell them about being "born again" or "born from above" and use John 3 and Jesus' conversation with Nicodemus.[22]

Questions for Chapter Eight:

1. What was the burden or major point in Chapter Eight?

2. How does Jonathan Edwards' sermon challenge you?

3. If you were to write out your B.C. (before conversion) condition, what would you say?

---

22 Jesus likened lost people to a lost sheep for which the shepherd searches in the thorny wilderness. The sheep has severed itself from the one who was its guide; it has removed itself from the fold, gone its own way and become lost. It is devoid of any bearings and without homing instinct (see Luke 15:4-7).

At other times, Jesus pictured lost people as patients on whom the doctor gives up (Luke 5:31); worse, like criminals on whom the sentence of death is carried out (Matthew 13:40-42). He compares their lostness to death (Luke 15:24), to destruction (Mark 12:9), to damnation (John 5:28-29). Jesus thus presents lost people as going astray and being condemned, lost in such a way that it requires more than that they simply be found; they must be awakened to eternal life and saved. https://www.cmalliance.org/about/beliefs/perspectives/lostness

4. Let's say your friend asks, "What's a 'biblical Christian'? What would you say from John 3?

5. If you are a "millennial" (someone born between the early 1980's to the late 1990's), you may have many friends who aren't committed to Christ. Do they know that you are? Are you praying that they will see a difference in your life?

A RESPONSE TO ONE-WAY FRIENDSHIPS

While sharing some of this information (especially my "Friendship Continuum" chart) with some veteran Christians, one leader said, "I can be a good friend to a lost person. But he can't be a good friend to me."

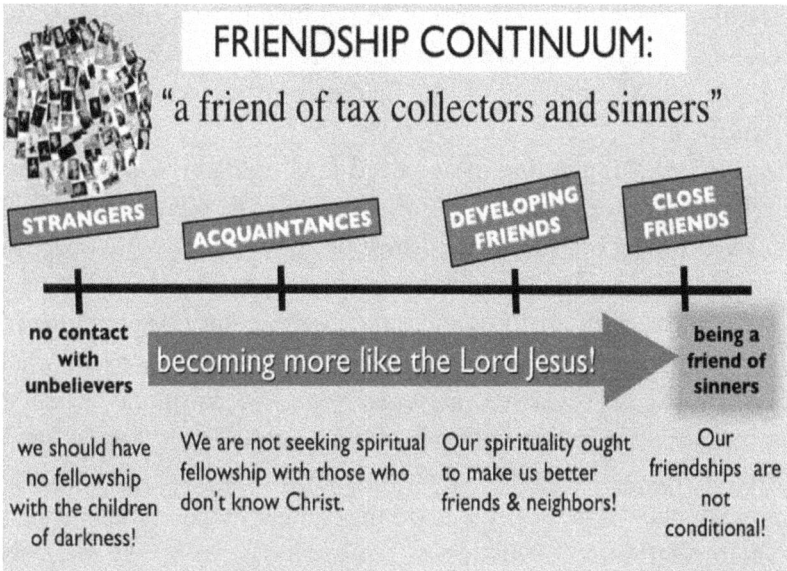

FRIENDSHIP CONTINUUM:
"a friend of tax collectors and sinners"

STRANGERS — ACQUAINTANCES — DEVELOPING FRIENDS — CLOSE FRIENDS

no contact with unbelievers

becoming more like the Lord Jesus!

being a friend of sinners

we should have no fellowship with the children of darkness!

We are not seeking spiritual fellowship with those who don't know Christ.

Our spirituality ought to make us better friends & neighbors!

Our friendships are not conditional!

When I asked what he meant, he said that there is no commonality between a child of God and one who is not yet there. "A saved person and an unsaved person have nothing in common," he stated. "As a believer I can offer much spiritual good to this lost person, but he has nothing to offer me."

I thought about that a bit. Jesus was a friend of sinners, but were sinners friends of Jesus? Did it matter to Him that He had those relationships? They had nothing to give Him, right?

A Lonely Adam

Part of being human is having significant connections with other human beings. In a perfect garden, before there was sin (and before Eve was created), we are told that Adam was "lonely" and that Adam's condition was "not good" (Genesis 2:18). He was in perfect fellowship with God — but he needed human companionship. If he needed human companionship in his not-yet-fallen environment, how much more do we in our broken world? We were not designed to have a relationship only with our Creator.

Let's think about several deficiencies in this kind of one-way friendship:

First, this is a denial of our need for human relationships. We can have significant and deep connections with members of God's family, but why not solid friendships with lost people? Are deep human friendships only possible between two saved people? (We will discuss some of the risks of these relationships in our conclusion).

In this regard, should only saved couples get married? Or is marriage also for those who are not yet in God's family? (Of course, we are not to be unequally yoked with unbelievers, and I would never perform a marriage ceremony for a mixed couple). But do we really believe that only Christians can get married? The deepest human relationship (outside of conversion) is not just for saved people. If lost people can have meaningful, serious relationships with other lost people, why can't the believer in Christ have such connections with those not yet in the family?

Second, we must emphasize (as we have throughout this book) that developing deep friendships with lost people is not for the purpose of spiritual fellowship. A personal relationship with Jesus is lacking in my unsaved friend. And it is the most important relationship there is! But it is not the only relationship that is important.

In this regard I am greatly moved by what happens in John 6. In that chapter Jesus has just fed the 5,000 with five small barley loaves and two small fish. He then launched into what we call "the

Bread of Life" discourse, claiming to be the manna God sent from heaven. He even says,

> 48 I am the bread of life. 49 Your ancestors ate the manna in the wilderness, yet they died. 50 But here is the bread that comes down from heaven, which anyone may eat and not die. 51 I am the living bread that came down from heaven. Whoever eats this bread will live forever. This bread is my flesh, which I will give for the life of the world."

As if those claims were not enough, Jesus then adds the following (incredibly provocative) statement:

> 53 Jesus said to them, "Very truly I tell you, unless you eat the flesh of the Son of Man and drink his blood, you have no life in you. 54 Whoever eats my flesh and drinks my blood has eternal life, and I will raise them up at the last day. 55 For my flesh is real food and my blood is real drink. 56 Whoever eats my flesh and drinks my blood remains in me, and I in them.

Many are offended at Jesus' cannibalistic-sounding claims, and walk away from Him. Jesus then asks His disciples in verse 67, "You do not want to leave too, do you?" Jesus wanted (and needed) the companionship of His disciples and expresses His desire that they not leave Him.

There is a linguistic feature in New Testament Greek that is significant here. Koiné Greek has a way of structuring a question so that the one asking the question is hoping for or anticipating a "No!" answer. The little negative **μη** is used.[23] So Jesus is really saying in verse 67, "You're not going to leave me too, are you? I hope not! Please say 'no'."

The truth is that the companionship of His disciples mattered to Jesus. And we have no reason to believe that they were all saved at this point. (Remember that Jesus even uses the term "friend" of

---

23   This is a common feature of the fourth gospel. Two additional examples in John are 4:29 and 8:53.

Judas Iscariot!). If connectiveness and relationship mattered to the Lord Jesus, how can it not matter to us?

Third, if we truly believe that our friendship with a lost person is only a one-way street (i.e., that we alone are the givers), we will have no significant connections with them. They will feel that they have nothing to offer us, that they are totally dependent on what we can offer them. But this is just silly. My lost friend who is a CPA can offer me great help with my taxes. My unsaved optometrist can give me a great eye exam. My lost friend who is as strong as an ox can help me lift my lawn mower into my SUV to get it repaired. My friend who understands politics can help me sort through the options this coming election. There is a world of information and skill and insight that my friends who are not yet believers possess, and I can benefit from a connection with them. Some of my friends have raised their children well, even though they have not focused on the critical spiritual dimension. Lost people, as well as believers, have access to what theologians call general revelation or common grace and we can benefit from their understanding. How dare we be so arrogant as to think that they have nothing to contribute in a friendship with us?

Fourth, Is salvation the only thing we offer our unsaved friends? As critical and essential as that is, doesn't friendship involve many other aspects? In our conversations, is the only topic redemption? We read in Mark 4:2 that Jesus "taught them many things." What makes us think that the only topic of conversation that we can have with lost people is their eternity? As a young believer I was taught to immediately go for the spiritual jugular, to steer any conversation to the issue of salvation and eternity. But what makes us think that we should not invest any time or energy into their BEFORE or their NOW? What I mean is, true friendship shows an interest in another person's history and their present circumstances.

Conclusion and Risks

As we attentively discuss a wide variety of issues with our lost friends, God will give us insight as to how and when we should bring up spiritual matters. And we can learn much from them about a myriad of issues. If they are into serious lawn care, we should show an interest in that topic. If they are excited about their child's athletic accomplishments, how dare we not rejoice with them and genuinely learn about their family? We must abandon the misguided idea of a one-way relationship. It is unbibilical and arrogant.

However, there are many risks which accompany the habit of developing deep friendships with lost people. We may conform to their lifestyle in order to advance the relationship. But believers *must not* compromise their Christian convictions for any reason. We may become silent in our witness out of fear of losing the relationship. But intense and serious prayer can open the door to sharing how our Christian faith meets us at the most practical levels of life. Lastly, we may lose the urgency of the gospel. No one will be saved simply by their friendship with a born-again believer. Conversion involves repenting for one's sins and personal faith in Jesus Christ. Careful, wise relationships should drive us to our knees to pray for openings to share a bit of God's truth with our friends.

A Survey of Friends Still "On the Way"

The burden of this book has been to encourage us believers to become friends of sinners like Jesus was. But what do our unsaved friends think of us?

So I decided to interview a few of my lost friends. As you can see from the email below that I sent them, I tried to word my request carefully so as not to be offensive. After you read through the interview request, I will give some of the comments I received from them with my brief response:

Dear __:

This is Larry Dixon. And I have a request. I'm working on a book that challenges committed Christians to develop deep relationships with those who might describe themselves as "still on the way" to faith or not convinced or not really interested in Christianity.

I hope you count me as one of your friends. And I mean no offense in contacting you. I think there are three groups of people: those completely committed to Jesus, those who are not there yet, and those who don't see themselves as moving in that direction. Your name came to my mind as someone whose opinion I value.

I'm looking to interview a few individuals who would say that they are not fully devoted followers of Jesus. Now if you are a fully devoted follower of Jesus, then this survey is not for you. But if you see yourself as someone who is, say, spiritually still on the way or for whatever reason you are not considering the Christian gospel, then I would appreciate your answering a few questions. This survey is not meant to be offensive. But sometimes Christians assume a lot about others that are not yet committed to Jesus. This is your opportunity *to express your opinion* and be honest in responding to the interview questions. I promise I will not use your name.

This survey, which can be completed in a few minutes, can either be done through email or in person. I would be glad to meet with you face to face if you prefer. I promise that your responses to my questions will be kept strictly confidential. Your name will not be attached to anything I put in my book. And I also promise that I will not pressure you in any way to become what I call a "fully devoted follower of Jesus." I simply want your opinion on a few questions.

Here are my questions:

1. Do you see yourself as "still on the way" in spiritual things or not yet convinced or not really interested in Christianity? Would you please briefly explain why you are where you are?

2. If you could put your finger on one problem or issue or question that is keeping you from moving from the category of not yet convinced to fully committed, what would that be?

3. What drives you nuts about those who say they are trying to be "fully devoted followers of Jesus"?

Thank you so much for your responses to this survey. It would be my honor to give you a complimentary copy of my book when it is published

Some Comments

No real names will be used. I sent out about 16 surveys, mostly to my tennis buddies or acquaintances from the past. I have high hopes that more will respond, but I've gotten six responses so far.

If you decide to send this survey out to some of your friends, be prepared to pay a cost. The questions raised in the survey, in a sense, force the person to ask where they stand with God. You might consider asking which friends would be willing to complete your survey before you send it out. Which I didn't do.

The responses I received ranged from one friend who replied to my survey with the words, "Sorry, Larry. I decline," to another friend who wrote about two pages' worth of response! You need to know that I have been a bit anxious for the past few days after sending out the survey. I try to be very careful and not be a pushy Christian. So I worded the survey as inoffensively as I could. Some might still be upset that I would ask such personal questions. I'm concerned how my relationships with some of those to whom I sent the survey will change. I hope for the better.

But I am writing a book and I do value their perspective! So, I'm doing *research!* Following are some excerpts from a few who responded to the survey plus my initial thoughts on how best to proceed.

All Suffer

One of my tennis buddies is a Hindu and he responded: "I was born as a Hindu but my life experience has showed [sic] me that one doesn't necessarily have to believe in one particular god or religion to be a good person. I believe that our ancestors invoked religion so that people will have hope." He went on to comment on how a positive attitude and hope are important to one's immune system (he's a physician). He also commented that "no matter what [a person's] religion or beliefs are," the same good things and bad things happen to people. "I have seen good people suffer and bad people thrive."

Perhaps an illness might move him in the direction of considering Christianity, he writes, but he is not sure.

To the question what drives you crazy about Christians, he says, "people who blame god for their misfortune"; religious people who live as hypocrites; and those who thank God for helping them win sporting events!

My Response:

I deeply appreciate my friend's response to the survey. I obviously have a lot of work to do to show my friend that Christianity is not just another religion constructed by man to explain good and bad things in life. I am praying for opportunities to follow-up with my friend.

Not Really Interested

A friend for whom I have prayed for twenty years, whose wife and two sons are believers, kindly took the survey. His answers were succinct. To the first question ("1. Do you see yourself as 'still on the way' in spiritual things or not yet convinced or not really interested in Christianity?"), he answered, "I am not really interested in Christianity because I am not yet convinced."

To the second question ("2. If you could put your finger on one problem or issue or question that is keeping you from moving from the category of not yet convinced to fully committed, what would that be?"), he responded, "I do not see the purpose of it for me, personally."

And to the third question ("3. What drives you nuts about those who say they are trying to be 'fully devoted followers of Jesus'?"), his response was: "Nothing drives me nuts, but the way my mind works, I have a hard time with the 'fully devoted' concept because I would not know when to stop if I was fully devoted."

My Response:

I am so grateful that my friend took the time to respond to the survey. Regarding his answer to the first question, I would ask him, "What would it take to convince you?" In other words, if by being "convinced" he means that he has solid evidence that Jesus is the only way to God, I would want to know what he would accept as evidence.

If someone says to you, "I'll only believe in God if He appears to me right now!", you might say that God hasn't said that He would do that. And, in fact, that would not necessarily be enough to convince some people. But God *has appeared* in human history in the person of the Lord Jesus. And it is to that historical event that we should point. What does the skeptic do with the historically reliable gospel accounts about Jesus?

My friend does not see the purpose of moving from the category of unbeliever to believer. But what if God has declared that there is only judgment for those who do not believe in Jesus? The fact that he doesn't see the purpose of a conversion to Christ means I have a lot of explaining to do about salvation. If he expresses an interest.

He says nothing about Christians drives him nuts, but he has a hard time with the "fully devoted" concept because he would not know when to stop if he were fully devoted. My response to that would be that the Bible, God's Word, should be his guide in what it means to be fully devoted. It does not teach that we should abandon our families, or go live in a cave, or stop eating meat and survive on locusts. True devotion in the Bible involves a heart that seeks each day to be submitted to Him, a will that bows before His will, and a mind that wants to learn the truths which God has given in His Word.

But my friend raises a critical question: How do we help people "get an interest" in spiritual things? Several principles help me here:

(1) We pray like crazy for them. We pray that God the Holy Spirit would bring a sense of conviction to their hearts that God is holy and they aren't and they are in a bunch of trouble!

(2) We live our lives before them as imperfect, but authentic, examples of God's forgiveness and grace. We won't do that all the time, but we can admit our mistakes and sins and receive God's daily forgiveness.

(3) When they are open to discussion, we can begin to raise questions about their present worldview. Dr. Francis Schaeffer said that such questions have the ability to remove the roof of their worldview from over their heads and allow the rain to pour in. Everyone has a worldview. We can challenge any worldview from the perspective of biblical Christianity — and trust God to bless our efforts.

Seeking to Reach the Theologically and Philosophically Trained Friend

How do we develop friendships with those who might have an extensive theological and philosophical background? What questions should we ask if we want to lead them into becoming fully-devoted followers of Jesus?

Several specific questions have helped me advance (sometimes only a little) in sharing the Christian gospel with such friends. Imagine that you have such a friend who says he or she is a fully-devoted follower of Jesus. What should you say?

Well, "Hallelujah!" is the first word that comes to my mind! But what if you suspect that their view of who Jesus is and why He came and how one can know God is vastly different from what you understand the Bible to teach? What then?

1. Ask the most fundamental question when it comes to a faith commitment and that is, "What is your final authority for what you believe?" Evangelical Christianity proclaims the Bible and the Bible alone is God's Word — and should have the final say-so for what we affirm (and for what we deny).

2. Don't hesitate to define your terms — and invite your friend to do the same. The Mormon, the Jehovah's Witness, and the Christian can all say the words "Jesus is Lord," but each means something vastly different from the other.

3. Don't shy away from the specific claims of the Bible about why Christ came, why He died, and what that can mean to someone who puts their faith in Him. Many religious people are good people, but in the final analysis no one can earn salvation by their goodness (review our discussion of the rich young ruler in Chapter Five). We who believe in Jesus dare not shilly-shally (vacilate) on the specifics of the Christian gospel. We will often have to wade through a mixture of various theologies and philosophies to find where God the Holy Spirit can help us connect with those exceptionally bright friends we have who are still lost.

Good to Go?

Another friend who kindly answered my survey made some very specific points about being a good person. He wrote, "The wording of your questions presume that you must be a Christian to be worthy of God's consideration to eternal life." He raises questions about the veracity of reporters today — and those of 2000 years ago. What is really important, he says, is summed up by his statement, "what really matters is you, as a person, [that's] what matters."

He also raises the question, if the answers (in Christianity) are so clear, why are there so many sects? "Why do we have sects within sects?" And on that issue, he apathetically says, "Who cares . . ."

He says that he is fully committed to religious values. He clearly believes in an afterlife. He shares that he tells departed family members every night that "I'll be with you soon."

Christianity is only 30% of the world's population, but it is "all I know." He then writes, "If God is a loving God, you are not going to have to have a password to get through those gates . . . your pass will be how you lived the life you were given." He then volunteered to write the intro for my book!

My Response:

I care deeply for this friend and grieve with him some of the tragedies he has experienced in life. I guess my first response would be to share about the exclusivity of Jesus' claims. He raises questions about whether the eye-witnesses to Jesus can be trusted, which is a legitimate question.

I would respond that the eyewitnesses do not contradict one another, are extremely careful to report the events of Jesus' life accurately (read Luke 1), and many of them paid for their witness with their lives (in martyrdom). If any ancient historical accounts can be believed, I would suggest, the writers of the four gospels deserve our affirmation.

I certainly agree that the fragmentation of Christian groups is a scandal. But that is true in every religion, is it not? The divisive and hypocritical lives of Jesus' followers does not negate the truth about Him (although such behavior does put a stumbling block in the way of those still on the way).

Christianity does not teach that all religions are simply different paths up to the same mountain top. Christianity's *exclusivity* is straightforward (as we read in Acts 4:12- "Salvation is found in no one else, for there is no other name under heaven given to mankind by which we must be saved."). To the question "Must one be a Christian to be worthy of God's consideration to eternal life?" one must humbly but unapologetically answer, "Yes! If the claims of Jesus are to be taken seriously."

My friend professes to be a believer in "spiritual things," but doesn't appear to go further than that. I am grateful that he wants to live a good and God-honoring life. But what about Jesus? Why did He come? What did His death on the cross accomplish?

I hope that my friend will read the fourth chapter of this book, for there we see that no one can be good enough to merit God's forgiveness. And that's why Jesus came.

A FEW IDEAS FOR THE LOCAL CHURCH

We have tried to make the case in this book for all of us believers to develop significant friendships with unbelievers. What role does the local church play in that commitment?

Well, we certainly can't be at church meetings every night of the week if we want to spend time with lost people. The leadership needs to model a life dedicated to cultivating serious friendships with lost people. Here are a few suggestions that church leaders need to consider:

1. The pastor and elders of the local church must teach the truth of being a friend of sinners from the Word of God. They must personally be convinced that this indeed is a practice we need to incorporate into our Christian lives. Teaching the truth of Jesus' love for sinners ought to give us a love for our lost friends.

2. The spiritual leadership of the local church should tell the congregation about the friendships they are working on without betraying confidences. No real names need to be given (God knows who those people are). Modeling a lifestyle of love for the lost is critical to the church developing an atmosphere of concern for those outside of Christ.

3. Leaders need to report on and challenge the church members to read significant books on friendship evangelism. Some titles that occur to me are:

— *Becoming Worldly Saints: Can You Serve Jesus and Still Enjoy Your Life?* (Michael E. Wittmer)
— *How to Give Away Your Faith* (Paul E. Little)
— *Out of the Saltshaker & Into the World: Evangelism as a Way of Life* (Rebecca Manley Pippert)
— *Questioning Evangelism: Engaging People's Hearts the Way Jesus Did* (Randy Newman)
— *Tactics: A Game Plan for Discussing Your Christian Convictions* (Gregory Koukl)

4. Start a neighborhood Bible study for seekers. A few years ago we started one at a local country club and entitled it "God, Etc." We were not charged by the club for the room we used and had several seekers attend. Stephen Brown tells about a Friday night gathering at his church that they entitled "Skeptics' Forum." Brown promised guests that they could ask any questions they wanted and would not be outnumbered by Christians. Some in your church may be skilled in apologetics. Encourage them to develop an outlet for their passion.

5. Promote at least one "seeker" event per year. When we lived in Canada, there was a church that I preached at once in a while. Every year they would have a "seeker event" which was a Valentine's Day Banquet. The tickets for that banquet went very quickly. The one rule of that church was that the church members could not attend that banquet unless they brought an unsaved couple with them! They asked me to speak at that banquet on one occasion. I asked, "How strong should I present the gospel at the banquet?" They said, "If hitting someone over the head with the Bible is a '10' and not mentioning Jesus at all is a '1', we would recommend a three." Your church does not have to be a "seeker" church to host one event per year that is focusing its efforts to reach the lost friends of church members.

6. We may need to rethink how we do church. Where are we providing space for church members to spend time with lost people? Where are we encouraging people to pray for their unsaved friends? I've been to too many mid-week prayer meetings that were nothing more than what I call "organ recitals" (we only pray for the health concerns of the members and sometimes go into great detail about their illnesses).

My passion is that church leaders would be renewed in their commitment to reach others with the gospel and that they would joyfully release the church to do things with those who need the Lord! The pastor and elders need to ask the congregation questions like: "What do you enjoy doing? What are some of your hobbies? What sports do you enjoy playing? Where might you connect with some of your lost friends and neighbors? Then go do it! Join that team. Become a member of that quilting club or Toastmasters' chapter! And we promise to pray for you!"

7. A film night with discussion or a debate between a believer and an unbeliever is another way to engage with those needing Christ. Such an occasion does not have to be held within the walls of the church to be blessed by God!

8. Have a game night at the church that is seeker-friendly. Or encourage your people to have a game night in their homes. Here's one card game that is a lot of fun and easy to teach. It is called "Big Boss/Little Boss."

Beginning Play with Big Boss/Little Boss

Have only one Joker in the deck. Each player draws a card from the shuffled deck to determine his respective rank within the game. The President holds the card with the highest number value, and sits at the table's forefront. The Vice President holds the second highest card, and sits at the President's left side. The Secretary/Treasurer player follows in descending card value order. The Gopher (sometimes called the Scum) player, holding the lowest-valued card, occupies the last available seat at the President's right side.

The Gopher shuffles the deck, distributing all cards among players. The President and the Gopher exchange two cards (the President must give up his two lowest cards, even if it is a pair; the Gopher must give up his two highest cards). There is only one Joker in the deck. The Vice President and the Secretary/Treasurer exchange one card each (the Vice President must give his lowest card to the Secretary/Treasurer and the Secretary/Treasurer must give his one highest card to the Vice President).

The President begins play by casting his first card (or cards — he can play a pair, etc.) and play moves clockwise. The next player must discard a card (or a pair, etc.) whose value trumps its predecessor's; if he cannot, he forfeits his turn and says "Pass." A pair must be followed by a pair. The Joker trumps any hand (even four of a kind).

The first player to get rid of his hand becomes the new President (and changes seats after the round). The second player to discard becomes Vice President, the third player becomes the Secretary/Treasurer and the last player to go out becomes the new Gopher (whose job it is to collect the cards and to deal the next hand).

Players tally points after each round. The President receives four points; the Vice President three points; the Secretary/Treasurer two points; and the Gopher one point. The first person to 40 points wins. Typically ten hands are played.

Some Hints:

If you are starting the round, it is best to discard your lowest cards first. If you have the Joker, play it to automatically win the next to the last round. Then you go out with the card you still have in your hand.

We played a Big Boss/Little Boss tournament when we lived in Canada. There were about ten tables set up, so forty people played ten hands each and then rotated to a new table. Great way to get to know people!

Other Games to Consider

I'm not a fan of board games like Carcassone or Settlers, but many other people are. We recently learned a game called "Dirty Marbles." Great fun! We also like to play a game with dominoes we call "Mexican Train." You can find the rules to Mexican Train here: www.mexicantrainrulesandstrategies.com